LEADING
WITH
VISION

BEESON
PASTORAL SERIES

LEADING WITH VISION

COMPILED BY
DALE GALLOWAY

Beacon Hill Press of Kansas City
Kansas City, Missouri

Library of Congress Cataloging-in-Publication Data

Leading with vision / compiled by Dale Galloway.
   160 p.; 23 cm. — (Beeson pastoral series)
  ISBN 0-8341-1724-X
  1. Christian leadership. I. Galloway, Dale E. II. Series.

BV652.1.L43 1999
253—dc21

00-0398

Contents

121636

Acknowledgments

This book has been a team effort. I am thankful for so many Spirit-filled friends and associates who helped put this vision-stretching resource in your hands.

Maxie Dunnam, John Maxwell, Elmer Towns, and James Earl Massey are pioneers whose ministries demonstrate the power of vision. Each of these contributing authors is a personal friend who has taught me much about how to lead with vision.

Neil B. Wiseman, professor of pastoral development at Nazarene Bible College in Colorado Springs, served as a pastor for 20 years before entering his current ministry of training pastors for a new century. Working from audiotapes and transcripts, he shaped the manuscript from presentations delivered at a Visionary Leadership conference I convened for the Beeson Institute for Advanced Leadership. Besides being a valued friend, he's a skilled editor, as you will soon discover. He's also the editor or collaborative author of a dozen other books.

Ralph Beeson, gracious benefactor of Asbury Theological Seminary, dreamed of new training environments that would develop whole new levels of pastoral leaders. His great vision underwrote and helped create one of the schools at the seminary, which in turn sponsored the Beeson Institute for Advanced Church Leadership and its inaugural Visionary Leadership conference. He is with the Lord now, but his vision is further extended through the pages of this book.

Maxie Dunnam, in his role as seminary president, has likewise been an on-campus champion of that dream. I am grateful for his advice, direction, and assistance in the creation of new endeavors like the Beeson Institute for Advanced Church Leadership.

Warren Bird, Penny Ruot, Brenda Hays, and many others on my staff played a significant role both in orchestrating the Visionary Leadership conference and in supporting various editorial and marketing personnel at Beacon Hill Press of Kansas City.

Kelly Gallagher, director of Beacon Hill Press of Kansas City, was instrumental in developing the idea behind the Beeson Pastoral Series, of which this is the first volume. He has been supported by Bonnie Perry, managing editor, and Bruce Nuffer, marketing director.

It is difficult to conclude an acknowledgments page, because so many additional people could be named. I must, however, express my gratitude to God for one more person—someone who has exercised the faith to dream big dreams with me for almost three decades: my enthusiastic wife, Margi.

Introduction

Why write another book on vision? Because, like a certain credit card, "you don't want to leave home without it."

All effective leadership begins with vision. Vision is seeing that which is not yet here—visualizing something before it is. Vision is the clear mental picture that leads people to reach out to the future. As Heb. 11:1, 6 says: "Now faith is being sure of what we hope for and certain of what we do not see. . . . And without faith it is impossible to please God."

Without vision a leader is like an octopus on roller skates: it goes everywhere and nowhere. As Rick Warren says, without vision people go "to another parish." Leadership without vision is like following an explorer without a compass. You don't know where you're going! Today's church desperately needs men and women who will be people of vision.

Willow Creek's Bill Hybels says that before a church can be grown it must first grow in the mind, heart, and soul of the leader. David Yonggi Cho, pastor of the largest church in the history of Christendom, often says that we must become "pregnant" with God's dream. It must live inside us. It must take over the inside of our being until God births it in our midst.

Nothing happens until someone dreams it, and without visions and dreams the church has no future. We partner with God through the Holy Spirit by bringing into creation that which is not yet here.

Vision is like the eye of an eagle. An eagle's powerful eyesight is something like eight times stronger than a human being's. An eagle can fly 300 feet in the air and see a nickel in three inches of grass. An eagle sees farther than most others see. It sees things others don't see. Today's church needs men and women who have vision like the eye of an eagle.

Vision enables you to soar beyond the mediocrity of doing the "same old, same old." You need the eye of an eagle to move beyond maintenance mentality to become a mission that makes a difference in your community by reaching people for Christ.

Vision works like a magnifying glass. If lined up with the sun and held still, it will burn a hole because of the way it can concentrate the sunlight. Similarly, vision from God gives focus so that the Son of God's power will come into focus.

Vision is also like the banks of a river. The borders of a river give direction. They take it with power to a destination. Likewise, vision keeps us moving in the direction God wants to take us.

This book on vision marks the launch of the Beeson Pastoral Series. Written by leaders for leaders, its distinctive quality will be the practical ways it addresses significant topics like vision. In the following pages, you will meet proven leaders whose ministries have demonstrated a contagious flavor of compelling vision. You will see why they are widely recognized as effective communicators. As a result, you will be challenged to trust God as never before and to seek Him for new ideas beyond what "you could ask or think."

The opening chapter, "The Incredible Power of Vision," frames the idea of vision. I used it as the opening presentation for a four-day conference I convened titled Visionary Leadership.

Next, James Earl Massey reminds you that the role of pastoral leader is one of dignity. His chapter, "Developing a Visionary Church That Has Integrity," will remind you of the great influence that can result when your vision is based on God's Word.

Chapter 3, by John Maxwell, likewise deals with the character of a Christian leader. "How to Be a Christlike Servant Leader" draws from the example of our Lord, showing how your leadership style can be both distinctive and inviting.

My presentation in chapter 4, "Seven Habits of a Visionary Leader," summarizes the key qualities I've observed in almost four decades of ministry. I want you to develop the heart of a champion pastor for the 21st century.

Once the vision begins to take shape, how do you get visionary leaders on board? You'll find great help as Maxie Dunnam addresses "Building Bridges, Rallying Support for the Vision."

Likewise, the next two chapters help you seek out, raise up, and train God's people for vision-driven ministry. John Maxwell focuses on "Discovering and Evaluating Visionary Leaders" while I address "Leading Visionary Leaders."

The final two chapters help keep the vision going in the right direction. Elmer Towns writes "Visionary Leaders Encounter Greatness." He wants lay leaders to maintain a consuming passion for Kingdom usefulness! "What Will Remain After You're Gone?" by Maxie Dunnam, challenges you to build for the future.

These nine pieces are like different facets on a diamond. Each one offers a different view of something powerful and beautiful.

It has been a joy and privilege to serve as executive editor for this volume. My prayer is that many of you will use this book as but one step in a lifelong journey of *Leading with Vision*.

If you'd like to join one of the training events for the Beeson Institute for Advanced Church Leadership, please contact my office and ask for a complimentary brochure or short video (see below). I believe God has called me to invest the next chapter of my life in training leaders, and it would be a privilege to deepen that relationship with you, the reader.

—Dale Galloway
Wilmore, Kentucky
Beeson_Institute@ATS.wilmore.ky.us
1-888-5BEESON

▪ *1* ▪

THE INCREDIBLE POWER OF VISION

Discovering God's Extraordinary Plan for Your Future

by Dale Galloway

An incredible vision launched the Early Church into effective world-changing ministry.

Scripture provides this inspiring report: "During the night Paul had a vision of a man of Macedonia standing and begging him, 'Come over to Macedonia and help us.' After Paul had seen the vision, we got ready at once to leave for Macedonia, concluding that God had called us to preach the gospel to them" (Acts 16:9-10). The passage shows how a vision produced such vigor and motivation that a group of people took immediate action because they concluded God was calling them. This passage, as paraphrased in *The Message,* underscores two bedrock benefits a clear vision provides: (1) "the dream gave Paul his map," and (2) "all the pieces had come together." I love those two sentences because they tell us vision moves us toward accomplishing our ministry goals and draws resources and people together.

Vision—the place where tomorrow is shaped—motivates ministry and determines achievement. Vision unleashes creativity and helps a body of believers visualize a magnificent future. Vision also serves as a catalyst for innovations and inspires passion for improvements. Vision provides an energizing force for a congregation even as it produces a picture of a faith-inspiring future that can be brought into being by individual and group actions, commitments, and priorities.

Tell me your vision and I can predict your future. Tell me your dream and I can tell you what your values are. Tell me your aspirations and I can predict the quality of your life. All this

11

means nothing happens in a church until someone seeks God's direction for that particular congregation. Breakthrough achievement in ministry always starts with a vision. Now that sounds so obvious, but unfortunately, only 4 percent of pastors have a vision for their churches, according to a research study by George Barna. That means 96 percent of Christian leaders need to dream more dreams and see more visions.

ision—the place where tomorrow is shaped—motivates ministry and determines achievement.

HOW IMPORTANT IS A DREAM?

In Prov. 29:18, the Bible tells us, "Where there is no vision, the people perish" (KJV). I was reading recently from John Haggai, who interpreted this verse to mean that without a dream, people throw off restraints. Everyone does whatever they want, like sheep without a shepherd. But with a vision, life has direction. Every day provides a new adventure in fulfilling our mission. With a vision, people tackle the impossible and frequently accomplish it.

Deep down within all of us is a need to make our lives count. That is the immeasurable value of a worthwhile dream. There is nothing like an all-consuming vision to give our lives the meaning for which we long.

Let's get a clear picture of typical congregational life. Without visionary leadership, a vacuum naturally exists. Then chaos follows as a church tries to do everything or nothing. But a soul-stretching vision as it inspires, energizes, and focuses a church shows a congregation a future that is better for individuals, for a church, and for the world.

An authentic vision does a church and its leader a lot of good by calling them to more effective ministry. A vision helps set standards of excellence, reflect high ideas, clarify purpose, set direction, inspire expectation, motivate commitment, and expand horizons. The significance of a vision is explained by management expert Burt Nanus in *Visionary Leadership:* "There is no more powerful engine driving an organization toward excellence and long-range success than an attractive, worthwhile, and achievable vision of the future, widely shared." A live church sparked with a magnificent vision grows and, as a result, usually experiences growing pains.

eep down within all of us is a need to make our lives count.

WHAT IS A VISION?

For the Christian leader, vision is faith bringing the future and the present together. In Heb. 11:1 we read, "Now faith is the substance of things hoped for, the evidence of things not seen" (KJV). I paraphrase the passage, "Faith is vision and vision is seeing a worthy possibility before it actually takes place." In fact, the whole 11th chapter of Hebrews is about persons who trusted God for things that seemed impossible to them or others. They had a dream for a great future. They saw something beyond what happened in the ordinary. Their faith gave them a vision of the future, captured their imagination, and mobilized their resources.

A vision is the ability, or the God-given gift, to see those things that are not as becoming a reality. The most miraculous things start to happen when church leaders get a clear-cut vision.

I have always loved those words of Jesus when He was getting ready to leave His disciples: "Anyone who has faith in me will do what I have been doing. He will do even greater things than these, because I am going to the Father" (John 14:12). That is an amazingly visionary promise—that we can do greater things than Jesus did. But because He said it, we can believe it is possible. It begins with a dream. George Barna says that for vision to be effective, it must be simple enough to be remembered but specific enough to provide direction. Bill Hybels believes before a church can be grown, it must be grown in the minds and hearts of a leader. Those are wonderful components of a worthy vision—great things, simple, easy to remember, specific, and believed by leaders.

David Yonggi Cho, pastor of the largest church in the world, located in Seoul, Korea, talks about getting pregnant with a dream, so it gets inside you and begins to shape and affect your whole being. I pray that you will become pregnant with a vision of what God wants to do through your ministry where you live. I pray, like an expectant mother, you will never be the same and can never get over the vision for your ministry, that you will see it big and lofty and noble. I pray you will get a clear focus and keep it simple so people can understand it.

Rick Warren, in his book *The Purpose-Driven Church,* suggests six ways to cast a vision: (1) Slogans or sound bites. I used slogans like "healing hurts," "building dreams," "follow the Cross to new hope in your life." (2) Symbols. We held classes for persons with various addictions. These classes represented our vision, they became a symbol of what we were about. (3) Scripture. (4) Stories. Over and over again have people tell the stories of what God is doing. That clarifies and inspires the vision. (5) Be specific rather than general. (6) Spend time with key leaders to help them positively use their influence.

I cherish the Book of Nehemiah because it is a book about dreams and faith. The contemporary church in some places lies in ruins, like the walls in Nehemiah's time. The people were discouraged, and the message had been disgraced. But after prayer and waiting before God, Nehemiah stood to cast a new vision. This is what he said: "You see the trouble we are in: Jerusalem lies in ruins, and its gates have been burned with fire. Come, let us rebuild the wall of Jerusalem, and we will no longer be in disgrace" (Neh. 2:17). He cast a vision. And you may ask, How often do you have to recast a dream in a church? Often—maybe every day. In the Book of Nehemiah, halfway through they got very discouraged. Nehemiah had to recast the vision—that was after only 26 days.

WHERE DO VISIONS COME FROM?

We have all known churches that spend lots of time formulating a long mission statement with some committee and never do anything with it. That is not the vision I am discussing. I have something much more dynamic, productive, and motivating in mind.

God wants to work through the function of our minds called *visualization* to accomplish His work on this earth. Great blessings come to us first by seeing. Consider how God worked with Abraham: "And he brought him forth abroad, and said,

Look now toward heaven, and tell the stars, if thou be able to number them: and he said unto him, So shall thy seed be" (Gen. 15:5, KJV).

The Father told Abraham to look up to the sky and count the stars, but those stars became countless. "Abraham, your seed, your descendants, will be as numerous as those stars," God said. In that moment, Abraham's eyes were filled with joyful tears as he saw himself becoming the father of a great nation.

> *It is not unusual for men and women who have God's vision to be thought crazy.*

We need to remember that until this time, Abraham and his wife, Sarah, had been barren. They had been unable to have a child and were now well past childbearing age. In fact, when Sarah first heard of Abraham's vision, she laughed out loud. It was ridiculous, impossible. She thought Abraham must be crazy. It is not unusual for men and women who have God's vision to be thought crazy.

In Acts 2:17, we learn that the Holy Spirit gives us visions and dreams: "And it shall come to pass in the last days, saith God, I will pour out of my Spirit upon all flesh: and your sons and your daughters shall prophesy, and your young men shall see visions, and your old men shall dream dreams" (KJV). Apparently dreams and visions are for everyone—young and old, men and women.

As we open our minds to the Holy Spirit, He plants the seed thoughts of dreams and visions in our minds and hearts. When you live in the land of visions and dreams with God, life is changed from ordinary to extraordinary.

Men and women of vision have no trouble praying because they have something to pray about.

Men and women of vision have no trouble sacrificing because they believe in something greater.

Men and women of vision have no trouble believing God for big things because they know that God can do the impossible.

Men and women of vision have no trouble with apathy because they know where they are going.

Men and women of vision find themselves setting measurable, realistic, inspiring, and attainable goals. They do not set easy goals that do not challenge faith.

Thus, our calling is to live the life of the Spirit and to be men and women of visions and dreams.

You create the church you will pastor in the future by the words you speak about vision today. Is it not interesting that churches actually experience what they speak? If you are around a church for a while and listen to what they talk about, you know what will happen. That is why a vision never comes to pass until someone sees it and begins to talk about it. That is what creates a faith community that believes God for the impossible. I believe nothing is impossible with God.

But before you can implement the vision God has for your church, you must take limits off your thinking. Many people have self-imposed, built-in limitations on their perspectives and their views of ministry. What I want to do is to take off all the hindrances, barriers, and glass ceilings. What I want you to do is to take the limits off your faith. Open up to God's big vision. Open up to the beautiful, all-consuming dream God is developing in you.

SEVEN STEPS TO TURNING A VISION INTO REALITY

B. N. Mills, quoted in *The Forbes Book of Business Quotations,* may not have been thinking about the church when he wrote these words, but he provides an accurate insight for our task: "Dreaming is just another name for thinking, planning, devising—another way of saying that a man exercises his soul. A steadfast soul, holding steadily to a dream ideal, plus a sturdy will determined to succeed in any venture, can make any dream come true."

Step one—dream a worthwhile dream. You have heard of the man who was out fishing all day and had not caught anything. Meanwhile, in a nearby boat were a man and woman who were catching many big fish. The first man couldn't keep from watching them all day long until it almost drove him crazy. What really tore him apart was that the couple threw the big ones back. Finally, because he couldn't take it any longer, he yelled, "How come you're throwing the big ones back?" The couple reached under their boat seat and pulled out a small frying pan. Then they answered, "'Cuz they won't fit in our frying pan."

Here is the message and meaning of this true-to-life parable: Everyone has a frying pan. Let's admit we have all thrown out a dream or an ideal because we thought it was too big. It just would not fit in our little frying pan. How sad to limit God by our small perspective and tiny faith.

There is a much better way. Let us begin to consider concepts and paradigms that help achieve new Kingdom accomplishments.

How do you test a dream to know if it is from God? When I was going to start New Hope Community Church, I considered four areas. (1) Would this be a great thing for God? (2) Would this help hurting people? (3) Will this bring out the best in me? Do I have the kinds of gifts to accomplish this vision? (4) Is this something that God is giving to me to do? Is this what God is calling me to do with my life?

> *How do you test a dream to know if it is from God?*

On October 14, 1972, my wife and I launched New Hope Community Church for the thousands of Portland, the most unchurched city in America. We started in a drive-in theater in Portland, Oregon, where it rains a lot. Margi and I climbed up the ladder on the snack shack roof. She sang and I preached. We bought a $50 microphone that would plug into the existing sound system. We had taped organ music that we had recorded on a reel-to-reel recorder. We had a person down inside the snack shack that had never been to church before in his life. He was a seasoned old veteran of the theater who had come and turned the sound on. And I can still hear my wife saying, in the middle of the service, "Art, that is the wrong song. Turn to the other song." It was a humble beginning—the only thing going for us was a big parking lot.

One Sunday I stood up and said, "Someday we will have hundreds of small groups all over this city led by dedicated laypeople. Someday we will have multiministries that meet people at the point of their needs. Someday we will have a 3,000-seat sanctuary on a lush green hillside, towering over the freeway system of this city. On top of that church we will have a cross, freestanding, illuminated, 100 feet in the air, and people will follow the cross to new hope in their lives."

Can you just hear a man in the car with his live-in girlfriend and dog in the backseat? He laughs out loud and says, "This preacher is crazy. I came out here to laugh at him." Does anybody laugh at your visions and dreams? If they are not laughing, maybe you have not dreamed big enough yet.

But that dream is what God helped us accomplish—a 3,000-seat sanctuary on a beautiful hillside, towering over the largest shopping center on the inside of the freeway in Oregon. I said to the architect, "Now our dream is to have a cross, freestanding, 100 feet in the air, so people will follow the cross to new hope in their life." He had problems with designing such a cross because of the winds, but he finally came through.

Many people have followed that cross, which is actually 108 feet high, to new hope in their life. Consider Wes, who came down the freeway one day. His wife had run off with his best friend. He was devastated. He had a serious addiction to drugs and alcohol. He was at the bottom. His will to die was almost stronger than his will to live. But Wes saw our cross. He got off the freeway and drove into our parking lot. It was Tuesday night; our Positive Singles group was meeting, and the singles' pastor invited anyone with a need to come forward for prayer. Wes went forward. Here came the small-group leaders, called lay pastors, in our singles group to pray with him. It did not stop there. They invited him back the next night to a Separation and Survival Group where they shared common pains and uncommon solutions. They brought him back the next night to a New Life Victorious Group for his alcohol/drug addictions. They brought him back on Sunday to hear a message about good news and hope.

Years had gone by when I ran into Wes as I walked down the hallway. He stopped me to say, "Pastor, tomorrow I graduate from college. You remember when I followed the cross to New Hope? Tomorrow I graduate from college, and I have a full-time job in alcohol rehabilitation."

I prayed later, "O God, what if on those days when I was standing out on the roof of that refreshment stand I had given up the dream? What about those days when I thought I would never survive? What if I had given up the dream?"

W hat is the vision in ministry God has given you?

Remember, the more worthwhile the dream, the more opposition and obstacles you may have to face. But do not give up the dream. It is a magnificent vision to which God has called us. It is what He wants to give you. So when the going gets tough, you get going and keep going.

What picture has God placed in your mind? What is the vision in ministry God has given you? The first step in seeing something beautiful become a reality is to get a clear-cut picture of the vision.

Step two—detail the dream. It is no accident—New Hope Community Church has the finest location any church could have because in those early days we did not just think it but inked it. Only 5 percent of people ever ink their vision. But a dream does not happen until you write it. You must detail it.

We wrote down our dream: "We want to be right off a freeway exit. We want to be on a lush green hillside. We want to be right along the freeway where thousands of cars that come up and down that freeway will see us. If we are going to build a church to reach this city, we must have high visibility. We want a property where the sewer is in and where the utilities are there so we do not eat up our money on that kind of cost. And we want to have 100,000 people within 15 minutes of that location." That is how we detailed the dream. That is exactly the kind of property we built on.

Think how you might build a balcony 50 feet high. You must build one step at a time to get to the goal. In a similar manner, you have to break your vision down into smaller, manageable parts. To make it happen, ink the vision—write the steps in detail to completing the vision.

Step three—dedicate yourself to the fulfillment of the dream. Someone has said dedication is the difference between a champ and a chump. I wish there were an easy way to build a church, but I have looked for an easy way all my life and there isn't one. There is no easy, no-effort formula that you can follow. Growing a church takes blood, sweat, and tears. It takes more dedication than anything else I know of.

John Meares, a caring friend of mine, pastored a great church in Washington, D.C., and now his son pastors the church. John was there for many years. Back in the '60s, all the Anglos fled to the suburbs and the congregation became mostly African-American. John, who is white, had his life threatened during the Washington riots. Sometimes men from his church slept in his front room so he and his family would not suffer bodily harm. One Sunday, in the middle of all this unrest, he was preaching and a group of gang members came in the back door to attack. The men in his congregation surrounded their pastor and threw the potential attackers out the back door. Pretty exciting and frightening service, wouldn't you say? When I heard this story, I asked John Meares, "Why did you stay there?" Tears rolled down his cheeks as he observed, "Because God gave me a vision for the inner city. God called me there. I dedicated my life to fulfilling that dream. That's why I stayed."

Why did John stay when others left? Because years before he had prayed through and had the assurance that his vision came from God. Thirty-four years later, he has an African-American congregation of thousands of people. And he has witnessed miracle after miracle as his people have moved from welfare to being successful in business, professions, and leadership positions in Washington.

Fulfilling the great dream God has given you takes a lot of dedication, but without wholehearted commitment your dreams are only empty wishes or passing fantasies. The vision is not going to happen until you get your heart in it. Jesus said, "Where your treasure is, there your heart will be also" (Matt. 6:21). What you place value on is going to have your heart. In the Bible the word *heart* means the center of your affections. To fulfill a great vision, you have to want it with all your heart.

Step four—dare to risk failure to gain success. Every time we moved to a new level of achievement at New Hope

Community Church, we had to make a conscious decision to take risks all over again. I used to have a picture of a turtle in my office with the caption, "He only moves ahead when he has his neck out." I do not know why, but the only times a church shows much progress is when it sticks its necks out a little further. But I would rather risk something significant for God and fail than do nothing and succeed.

Think about the children of Israel standing at the Red Sea. They were scared. As they looked back, they could see the chariots approaching in a cloud of dust. Pharaoh was bringing all of his army and the Red Sea was in front of them. In Exod. 14:15, "The LORD said to Moses, 'Why are you crying out to me? Tell the Israelites to move on.'" Look at the Scripture and their situation. When do you think the waters parted? When they moved forward? When they put their feet in? When the waters were knee high?

For years Moses prepared and got ready. In Exod. 14 we see that as a result of the 10 plagues, the children of Israel were on the march out of bondage when they came to the Red Sea. Suddenly they were frightened. Before them was an impossibly huge body of water. Behind them was the heavily armed Egyptian army. "What shall we do?" they cried out in panic.

And when Moses gave the command, God used his words to create a miracle. The sea was parted and the Israelites marched through the open sea to safety on the other side.

Right after World War II, the two giant retailers in America made two very different decisions affecting their separate destinies. One was the Sears Roebuck Company while the other was Montgomery Ward.

The leadership of Ward's expected that after the war an economic depression would come, so they refused to take any risk in expanding. Meanwhile, the leadership of Sears determined that there was going to be economic growth such as America had never seen before. So they went out and expanded into new markets all over the world. As a result, Sears soared ahead while Ward's fell far behind. Sears risked failure, and thus gained greater success.

I am not advocating irresponsible, reckless risk, but I am talking about faith-based risk. After doing all the research and seeking the best counsel possible, there comes a time when you have to go for it. If you ever stop going for it, then you stop being effective for God. Success is a process.

Step five—focus on your dream. So many people never achieve much in their life because they scatter in all directions. To fulfill a great vision takes singleness of mind. It has been said that what gets your attention gets you. To fulfill a vision, you must concentrate on the fulfillment of the vision.

This is a confusing time in contemporary society. Ministry has changed more in the last 10 years than ever before. It continues to change rapidly, and so many things bid for people's attention. Only a clear vision from God will keep a pastor and congregation focused on what really counts. Without a vision, you will toss to and fro. And you will wonder what ministry is about at the end of every day.

o fulfill a great vision takes singleness of mind.

If you are going to achieve your dream, it is going to take a lot of concentration. It is going to mean denying lesser things to gain this greater vision. Jesus is our pattern—He stayed focused on His mission; nothing could distract Him from His purpose.

Step six—determine to fulfill your dream. A primary reason why so many never achieve their dream is that they give up when they suffer a little setback. In the 6th chapter of Nehemiah, the leader had his life threatened. His enemies were undermining his reputation. I am inspired by Nehemiah's reply: "I am doing a great work and I cannot come down. Why should the work stop while I leave it and come down to you?" (v. 3, NASB). Determination is the ability to stay on the wall and turn the vision into reality.

I believe that I have some gifts for ministry, but I know my gifts are not greater than many other pastors'. But God has given me a determination to stick with a God-inspired dream. I can go for the long run and do whatever it takes, day after day, week after week, month after month, year after year. I am determined to see my vision accomplished.

Columbus encountered a terrible storm as he crossed the Atlantic. Some think his ship traveled about two miles an hour.

He had lots of vision testers and dream doubters. All aboard his ship thought the earth was flat. The sea was rough. The crew was seasick and frightened. They nearly mutinied.

But Columbus and his vision persevered. Someone wrote about Columbus, "Brave admiral, what do we say when all hope is gone? Back come the words like a leaping sword, 'Sail on, and on, and on, and on.'" That is the intensity of determination we need to build great, growing, healthy churches.

Step seven—put your faith into action. Visions verbalized in words of faith release the creative powers of God to work through our lives and ministry. Early in our ministry of New Hope, God gave me a burden for single people. I envisioned that we would have a great need-meeting ministry. I shared this consuming vision with my friend and fellow pastor, Rich Kraljev, and it became his vision. For months we prayed together about the launching of this vision.

On Easter Sunday, 1977, knowing that God's timing was then, we launched the Positive Singles ministry. Without any people, we visualized and spoke the words of faith by advertising in the *Oregonian* the following: "100 Christian Men at New Hope's Positive Singles." Then we gave the time and place. We not only visualized that we would have men, but we spoke words of faith based on the assurance in our hearts that this was what God wanted.

This principle was also evidenced with the completion of our 3,000-seat auditorium constructed in less than 12 months. In cooperation with the Holy Spirit, we spoke words of faith and participated in the creation of a marvelous miracle.

I want to clarify this point. You should not just stand up and say something, expecting it to happen automatically. That is not faith in action—that is foolishness.

And of course, there is an incubation period, just as a period of time must pass before a baby is born. Spend time with your vision in fellowship with the Holy Spirit, clarifying, crystallizing your dream. Purify your motives and desires, and make sure that God wants to use your life to make this thing happen. Pray through and get the assurance that this is God's will for your life. Then, like Moses of old to whom God gave the vision to deliver

the children of Israel out of Egypt, take the directions that God
has given you. Speak the words and lead the people.

FUEL YOUR VISION WITH PASSION

As we have seen, vision is seeing that which is not yet
here—visualizing something before it is realized. Researcher
George Barna in his book *The Power of Vision* clarifies the issue
very clearly for me: "Vision for ministry is a clear mental image
of a preferable future imparted by God to His chosen servants

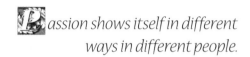

*assion shows itself in different
ways in different people.*

and is based upon an accurate understanding of God, self, and
circumstances." What strikes me as odd is how often people describe their dreams but do not apply an all-out, intense combina-
tion of their commitment, giftedness, life experiences, and faith.

I strongly believe that if our vision comes from God, we will
have both preparation and a passion for it. In fact, passion fuels
vision. If we do not have the emotional fire and heartfelt enthusiasm known as passion, we won't have true vision.

Passion shows itself in different ways in different people.
One common thread that I have seen in every great and cutting-
edge church is this: a passion to reach the lost for Christ. If you
do not have passion to share the gospel with those who need it,
you will not have vision that matches God's priorities.

HOW TO CULTIVATE, REFUEL, AND INCREASE PASSION

Would you like to cultivate greater spiritual passion for
your vision? God stands ready to supply the motivating drive we
need in the following ways:

1. Passion often comes out of where a person met God.
People who found Christ through New Hope Community
Church when it met in an outdoor, drive-in theater tended to
have a passion for helping the drive-in ministry succeed. Someone who came to Christ in a small group often shows a passion
for small groups.

2. Passion comes from our quiet times with God. As you
walk with God, do you continually ask yourself, "What would

Jesus do in this situation?" or "How would Jesus feel now?" Are you passionate about what Jesus cares about?

3. Passion is contagious. I have a videotape from Bill Hybels on his vision for Willow Creek Community Church. He shares his unashamed passion for evangelism, the "fire that burns in [his] bones" (Jer. 20:9, TLB) for seeing every unchurched Harry and Mary in Metro Chicago come to Christ and then become fully devoted disciples. I cannot watch that video without having my passion rekindled.

4. Passion comes by taking time to dream. You could take a real vacation. Or go to a conference. For many years, my wife, Margi, and I journeyed to the Robert H. Schuller Institute for Successful Church Leadership. There at the Crystal Cathedral, we heard pacesetters who had dared to dream a great dream for the glory of God through the expansion of His kingdom. These gifted communicators inspired their hearers to think big. We left invigorated with the power of God and renewed in our passion to be difference makers.

5. Passion increases with continual surrender. I remember a friend confronting me about my response to a painful disappointment. "Dale, you're bitter," he said frankly. He was right. I needed to learn that surrender to the Lordship of Jesus included not only my will but also my pain, ill feelings, rights, and whatever else would dilute my passion from what God had called me to do. Maintaining a focused passion is impossible without a sense of continual surrender to letting the Holy Spirit direct my life. There is no accomplished mission without surrender.

Putting It All Together

In a December 1997 *Leadership Network* forum, Peter Drucker and Lyle Schaller served as principal resource leaders. Dr. Schaller helps us with passion: "The critical issue in society is a shortage of competent leadership with the kind of passion that generates followers. This is also the critical issue for churches. What in our congregation are you doing to produce passionate leaders for the next generation?" And what are we doing to increase our own passion?

The sooner you and I identify, cultivate, and increase a passionate vision for things that matter to God, the more He will unleash a clear vision for the future in each of us. At New Hope Community Church, we often spoke of the desperate need to reach the unchurched thousands in greater Portland. When my vision behind those words was compelling, then God seemed to use us to make the greatest impact. Nothing is more powerful than when God's people led by a Spirit-filled leader come together with passion that makes their visions and dreams become a miraculous reality.

2

DEVELOPING A VISIONARY CHURCH THAT HAS INTEGRITY

The Cornerstone of Our Dream for the New Century

by James Earl Massey

The Church began under a leader with the highest integrity: Jesus of Nazareth, a teaching preacher. Intent on developing an effective working group for ministry in the world, Christ fashioned a community that looked to God, trusted His judgment, and had eyes of vision for claiming the world. Our Lord planned the Church intentionally based on truth. He founded the Church in order to have a community with integrity to continue His work in the world when He went back to be with His Father.

The Christian minister must always remember how the Church began. He or she must know what the purpose for the Church was in the mind and heart of the Founder, so that we can follow the same lines of integrity by which Jesus established the Church. In our contemporary American setting, I am wary of the business model as the best image for the pastor because it smacks of commercialism and capitalism. The Bible's focus is on the Church as a fellowship, a family, and a functioning community. And the pastor leads such a functioning fellowship built on integrity and energized by truth.

JESUS INSPIRED VISION BY TEACHING TRUTH

I said that the Church began under the ministry of an itinerant teaching preacher. The emphasis on teaching was very strong in His ministry because He knew that those who came to hear Him needed truth—truth about God, truth about life. And He shared that truth with them. In fact, so filled was He with truth

27

and so fully shared He the truth that He came to be known as the Truth, as well as the Way and the Light. In His teaching, His major method for developing this community, He was masterful and so engaging that those who heard Him gladly called Him Rabbi, my master. He taught Truth.

Again and again in the Gospel accounts, when persons were addressing Jesus in the midst of His teaching, they referred to Him as Rabbi or Teacher. According to the account in the Gospel of Matthew, the crowds were astonished at His teaching. It might very well be that in our day, teaching does not seem to have the kind of allure, the kind of attractiveness, that we read about in the New Testament on the part of Jesus. But when the Church began, it began around the central figure of a teacher of truth.

NEW TESTAMENT LEADERS FOLLOWED THE PATTERN OF JESUS

The New Testament writings reflect the fact that this spirit of teaching was not only in Jesus, who founded the Church, but was also at work in the life of those who continued His ministry when He went to be with God. This spirit of teaching was strong in the churches during the first century for two reasons. First, Jesus as the Founder of the Church had been a teacher come from God, and this kept the teaching ministry in continuing esteem. Second, the Church leaders Jesus appointed to continue His ministry knew that sound living, or living with integrity, depends upon sound teaching.

> *When the Church began, it began around the central figure of a teacher of truth.*

John Knox, who taught for many years at Union Theological Seminary in New York City, wrote a special essay many years ago for a volume titled *The Ministry and Historical Perspective,* one of three volumes published in order to highlight theological education. In this specialized article, Knox commented, "The fact that Jesus is characteristically known as a teacher must reflect not only the original fact but also, in some degree, the importance of the teacher's role in primitive Christianity."

The early teachers of the Church planned strategically. They intended to guide the awakened intellect, to provide religious answers for the questioning mind, and to offer a systematized body of truth for the questing soul. The teaching reflected and reported in the New Testament writings mainly involved believers—yes, persons already won to the faith through the preaching of the gospel. But the Epistles also show that what is taught was necessary as follow-up to what is proclaimed. The soundest basis for church growth is not merely to proclaim, but to teach. Teaching the full implication of the proclamation helps to develop a church that has integrity.

By the time the Pastorals were written, it was expected that those who chose to be pastors would be able teachers (1 Tim. 3:2). In fact, the stipulations regarding pastoral ministry made teaching an imperative function. Henry Sloan Coffin, who was the dean at Union Theological Seminary at the time John Knox was teaching, said, "A preacher who would minister in the same pulpit for a quarter of a century, or at least for a decade, and would train a congregation in conviction and ideals, in methods of intercourse with the Unseen, and in ways of serving the commonwealth, must follow a similar educational system as was followed by the Apostles."

In the New Testament, teaching is highlighted far more acutely than leadership. Then authentic leadership was provided the church through teaching the truth about God and life.

Given the unique history and posture of American society, no professional role has been more strategic to social progress than that of the teacher. And I would think that our society is in great disarray in our time largely because the teaching profession has been undermined.

This has also affected what happens in our churches. Teaching is not always valued. The founding and continuing development of the nation's churches, together with their strategic impact upon the development of the character of the nation during this several hundred years' experience and experiment in democracy, has depended in great measure upon the work of ministers who could teach. But we are, I fear, weakening or altogether deserting our ministry of teaching.

VISIONARY LEADERS ARE TRUST OFFICERS OF TRUTH

As a servant leader in the church, the minister shares status and authority with many others who are called and commissioned to be trust officers in the service of the Lord. We are called and commissioned to share and pass on the charismatic message about salvation and to train believers in the values and implementation of this good news from God. You and I as ministers are expected to teach what the church has always taught. In this service, we must follow the lead of the first Christian preachers and teachers, whom Albert Outler aptly described as "traditioners, trust officers of the Christian treasure of truth, qualified judges of right teaching."

As ministers, leaders of churches, you and I not only identify the tradition of which we are a part but also are identified with it and by it. When you and I stand to serve, we are standing and serving as trust officers who share the truth.

We are passing on something that is not novel or new. It is something that was here earlier. It was established by our Lord, and it must continue with integrity. Teaching is one of the strongest ways by which that integrity is passed on by way of concept and identification.

The Christian gospel is God's invitation to an experience, an experience inclusive of moral effects, spiritual effects, and social effects.

In our New Testament, we find the initial record of that experience as it is registered in the lives of distinct persons whose memory we hallow and whose names we continue to honor. But that biblical record is also the sourcebook for the kind of noble, serious, instructive, and necessary work that we must do as teachers. It is from within this province of the distinct biblical record that the Christian minister is expected and authorized to teach what the church teaches.

VISIONARY LEADERS ARE SHAPERS OF COMMUNITY

Along with teaching, pastors are expected to inspire and promote what generates social uplift and human advancement through freedom, justice, fairness, and the steady pursuit of community, which has been lost. Very little notion of the values of community are being rightly espoused in our time. We are privatized now in America. We are tribalized. We are competing. If this loss is to be turned back, it must be turned back by those of us who understand why the tradition was established and what it is intended to do in succeeding generations.

I don't know whether or not you view yourself as a teacher, but if you want to have a church that has integrity, it will have to come and be maintained by the method our founder used—teaching. Linked by calling and tradition to the event in the message of Jesus Christ, we are expected to be a servant of God's Word to the world, teaching what the church teaches.

We are sharers in that grand and great succession of those who have dared to proclaim the Christian faith, those who have dared to interpret the Christian faith, and those who are seeking to fulfill the implications of the Christian faith. And you and I

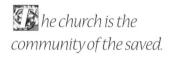 he church is the
community of the saved.

are linked by life and experience with people who are struggling to survive, who are trying to achieve in a secularistic and otherwise problematic society; and the best tool we can give to people in order to struggle well and aptly is truth, which is communicated through teaching. By teaching truth, we apply the insights of the faith and encourage people, uplift people, and guide people, after we have won people.

A church that has integrity must begin at the point of someone taught about the meaning of salvation. The church is the community of the saved. How are they saved? Through hearing the message of truth from the preacher. It is interesting how much Paul linked salvation with the messenger that brings the news regarding it. It is a truth handled, taught, shared, lived, advocated, modeled—integrity. Developing a church that has integrity by means of experienced truth must be at the core of our concern.

THE VISIONARY IMPACT OF PREACHING

First among the strategic means for this teaching that I am holding to your view again, is the ministry of preaching. Preaching rightly understood allows moral and spiritual instruction to be shared in mass fashion. It allows truth to be shared in a popular medium, but always with an individual impact.

According to the Synoptic Gospels, there was a blend between preaching and teaching in the ministry of Jesus. (There are passages in the Gospels in which the terms "preaching" and "teaching" are used interchangeably so that the action of Jesus in addressing His hearers in public appears pointedly didactic and declarative at one and the same time. As you review the Sermon on the Mount as told by Matthew and then by Luke (which is much shorter), you see the blend of teaching and preaching in the Master's life. Jesus instructed in order to inspire. He gave content in order to share comfort. He declared at the same time that He explained.

Understanding is always imperative for those who seek to live out their faith and aptness in relating biblical truth with personal questions, and the needs of people keep the teaching minister linked with them as an essential helper of their faith.

This accent on teaching is part of the pastor's role, as I indicated from 1 Timothy, chapter 3, verse 2, which requires the pastor to be an able teacher. This was highlighted in the first century, and the Church grew by leaps and bounds. It must return to our concern if our churches are to grow by leaps and bounds with integrity. This readiness and skill to instruct must be reflected when the congregation gathers to worship God. It must be there when they are addressed out of God's Word—teaching through preaching.

True religious experience is more than an emotional mood. Today there is a great deal of entertainment in the midst of our worship. People view the excitement of the occasion as a clue to the vital happening, but unless something is being taught and caught, the integrity is missing.

THE VISIONARY EFFECT OF DOCTRINE

The climate of modernity does not inspire faith, although it does press persons to seek and locate a faith. Preaching in mass fashion calls attention to the Christian faith, and it does so by isolating certain facts and certain truths from inside the experience of that faith. So preaching that is religiously instructive must address matters of doctrine. Charles Spurgeon once said,

"The most fervent revivalism will wear itself out in mere smoke if it is not maintained by the fuel of teaching." Sound teaching precedes sound living.

The concern to share doctrine must be a part of our passion—not doctrine for doctrine's sake, but for the sake of the people's understanding and for the use of faith by which to live rightfully. Doctrine is best focused when the way it can help has been

 *iblical doctrines matter for life at its best.*

understood first by the preacher. It then breeds life, and imparts a liveliness. It shows itself in more than an abstract subject, and it claims attention as a necessary message that attracts, alerts, and assures. The earnest preacher will seek to make the most correct statement of the truth with which he or she is dealing, the most correct statement with which we are dealing at the time. But that statement must be pertinent to the needs of those who are to hear it. To merely preach doctrine is not enough. We must understand the implications of the doctrine for the lives of our people and for ourselves. This is the way integrity is developed in a congregation.

Biblical doctrines matter for life at its best. When somebody says, "I don't want any doctrine," they do not understand the importance of shared truth. Doctrines rightly understood, rightly shared, satisfy the soul's quest for truth, and they liberate the mind by engaging the thoughts. What a marvelous thing to leave the sanctuary at the close of a worship service and for someone to say to you, "I've got something to wrestle with this week because of what you shared this morning." The preaching that really matters does not separate inspiration from something that has been taught.

Howard Thurman used to tell about how impressed his grandmother was with the preaching that she, a former slave, had heard from a certain slave minister when she was a girl. The slave preacher was allowed to come to the plantation and preach about four times a year, and on each occasion he had drilled into the consciousness of all of his hearers the notion that they did not have to feel inferior because they were slaves. As Thurman used to tell it, everything in him quivered with the pulsing tremor of raw energy when in his grandmother's recital, she would come to the triumphant climax of the slave minister's message because he always ended the message the same way. "You," he would say, with his eyes fastened upon them, standing his full height, six feet tall—"You are not niggers. You are not slaves. You are God's children."

That kind of sharing of truth gave a people a grounds for personal dignity. Preaching that does not involve the sharing of truth at the level of human need is not what brings the church integrity. It is out of that profound sense of being children of God that the slaves could handle the pressures of their days. The idea that they were children of God was not something that the slave masters shared with them. They were subjects and cattle to the slave owners, but the preacher gave them that bedrock truth that brought them through. That is the foundation of the African-American faith. We must call the church back to this kind of level of understanding of who we are because of God's mercy and God's grace. We must share it.

The white preacher who served the master's interest always taught them, "Slaves, obey your master." That was the bulk of the training that the slave master's preacher sought to convey. He argued his doctrine defensively, intent to keep the people submissive. But the slave preacher applied his doctrine in the interest of his hearers. He sat where they sat. He felt what they felt. And he was intent to liberate their spirits. That is the true function of sound teaching: to liberate people. You shall know the truth, and the truth shall make you free.

THE VISIONARY IMPACT OF PASTORAL CARE

Pastoral counseling ranks among the central services a minister is expected to make available to those who seek it. We teach by counseling. Our effectiveness in counseling will depend upon many factors, of course, but the ability and the readiness to share insights and perspectives in dealing with persons who need help cannot be overemphasized.

Wayne Oates, one of the great and grand traditionalists of his profession but also a great human spirit touched by God, listed several levels within the field of pastoral care, and one of those levels is that of teaching. As interpreters of the Scriptures and as ordained servants of the church, you and I must share perspectives that are of an instructional value, in spite of all the other theorists who insist that we cannot go about it that way. The necessity to instruct seems very clear when dealing with persons whose moral views are problematic, whose religious views are heretical, whose attitudes are unhealthy, and whose experiences need some clarifying conversation. It calls for instruction on our part as we counsel.

This religious care of troubled persons in our time must include the need to share information and insight, as well as a caring presence. The minister's counsel will be given to share insights, rehearse meanings, answer questions, resolve conflicts, appeal to motives, heal inward injuries, stimulate faith, purge the soul, promote change, provide emotional release, encourage persons to venture, and grant them enablement by which to move ahead on their own. Rightly done, the counsel that you and I share by means of our teaching can clarify life for the counselee and help the person handle the confusion that experiences often bring. All of us can think of persons who have come to us, so direly confused that even we hardly knew where to begin in seeking to help them. When the counsel is instructive, inspirational, and supportive, it helps center a person in order to make a wise and informed decision and to act in a way that counts. This is what I mean by integrity.

In light of the minister's need to serve such ends and to serve them well, sound training for this kind of work is a must. Most seminaries rightly require ministers to prepare themselves for this through courses in pastoral care and counseling. Quite beyond the notion of counseling, there must be an understanding of truth by which to counsel properly.

THE VISIONARY IMPACT OF GUIDED STUDY

Another way by which we can help our church develop integrity is to teach a class in the church program. Given this teaching responsibility that devolves upon the trained minister who pastors, and given the investment of years of study in this ministerial role, it is not too much to expect the pastor to view the congregation as a school in Christian living and labor. The congregation comes to school whenever we are having worship. The congregation comes to school whenever we are studying in a formal way. And when that happens, the pastor ought to have a very special, up-front role in the teaching process. Passing this off to someone else does not help a congregation coalesce around its leaders.

> *he congregation comes to*
> *school whenever we are*
> *having worship.*

I know some of you regularly teach a pastor's class that involves new converts, new members, young people, or children. This approach is fine, but it is better to engage the entire congregation in guided study if you can, either to examine a biblical theme or some biblical book or some issue in life from a biblical perspective with the minister as the teaching elder. I do not think the Presbyterians have it wrong at that point. They highly emphasize that teaching role of the pastor. But whether we do this with the whole congregation or within a small group from the congregation, this face-to-face approach as an involved teacher of the people permits a sense of partnership in learning, a sense of togetherness in being under the authority of the Word of God.

Adolf Schlaughter, great German theologian of another day, had delivered a great sermon, in the eyes of a person who greeted him after the service was over, and she said, "Sir, I'm glad to meet a theologian who stands on the Word of God."

He said, "I understand what you mean, but I want to correct you at one point. I do not stand on the Word of God, I stand under it." When the pastor does this sort of teaching, the congregation is reminded that integrity comes by being under the authority of the Word of God.

This fundamental work of the minister in the congregation of believers is to share the Christian faith, interpret its significance for all of life, and develop a Christian consciousness, which is sadly missing in many of the churches that are growing.

TEACHING TO BUILD A
VISIONARY CHRISTIAN CONSCIOUSNESS

In our time, there is a consumer consciousness, but not a Christian consciousness. Out of this Christian consciousness, agape love flows, the love that accepts people where they are and treats them there as if they were where they ought to be. The concerned minister will be alert to the need for resources, methods, and occasions for fostering this ordered approach to this perennial task, always eager to affect greater competency in this necessary work of the church.

I remember when I was given the charge of pastoring in Detroit. In the first business meeting that we held as a congregation, I asked them for permission to use the first three hours of every morning free from any encumbrances apart from an emergency that might arise, and I told them why. I told them I wanted to be in study, preparing for worship, exegeting passages so that I could gain the meaning of Scripture to share with them for their living, and I said, "I want to spend time in prayer so that when I come among you in my visitation at the hospital or in your home, my presence will count for something. It will be more than routine."

I was fresh every Sunday and never had burnout.

They agreed to give me the first three hours of the early morning free from any encumbrances, and that lasted for 25 years. I was fresh every Sunday and never had burnout. I am talking about a way of staying vital by means of being under the truth and scheduling times in such a way that our main business remains the main business. As a result of what happened in the midst of that kind of commitment, we did not have room for the people who came to Bible study in the midweek hour. They were standing around the walls—teaching, teaching—sharing truth. A church develops integrity by being in touch with truth, where everyone sees himself or herself in that mirror, and so we know how we look. And we can appeal to God for change. Integrity.

VISIONARY IMPACT OF A HOLY EXAMPLE

By attitude and behavior, a pastor incarnates what the church is to be and how growth will take place. A pastor develops integrity most contagiously through his or her own personal Christian character and earnest example. The accent I am placing upon a personal life that can appeal to others is very important because unless we instruct out of a sense of integrity that is granted by the graciousness of the Lord, unless we do our work out of a disciplined direction by being under our Master in heaven, then whatever we do will not matter anyway. The character and the ability of the person in the pulpit will determine the nature of its work and the extent of its helpfulness.

Harold Carter—pastor in Baltimore, Maryland, well-known scholarly preacher whose education for ministry was gained at several of the leading theological seminaries in our country—commented in print some years ago: "I never heard the instructor in Christian ethics lecture on the basic morality that ought to be part and parcel of the Christian ministry." During any class in ministerial ethics, this should be consciously and intentionally done so that we understand the meaning of being a minister of the Word.

Aware that this need for moral character is so important and necessary that it should not be overlooked or left unmentioned, Carter devoted a whole chapter to this subject in his book *Myths That Mire the Ministry*. He warned against concupiscence, which he defined as that desire for temporal ends that has its seat in the senses. He further said, "Sex presents such a formidable problem in ministerial ranks, and since this is so, an in-depth study of its impact on our calling would be a blessing in seminary circles." Many seminaries now include the study of human sexuality among their required courses so we can understand our humanity and how to discipline it for the sake of integrity as we lead.

Now, some of those studies that are presently being offered include an inquiry into the problem of sexual promiscuity as not only a failure in morals—which it is—but sometimes a behavior disorder or an addiction. Male and female seminarians taking these courses are guided in studying themselves existentially, with a focus on understanding temptation, entanglements, the influence of moods, the problem of viewing other persons as objects, and the problem of a low self-esteem that manifests itself in seeking to control other people. And none of these things, on the part of the minister, can help him or her minister with integrity. We must come back to that biblical notion of holiness, which in the Greek really means wholeness. We must be of one piece.

Given the scope and the import of ministering, a serious look at our own selfhood and the potential problem areas about which we must be aware is increasingly necessary. The ultimate response that vital ministry demands of you and of me is that of a God-committed selfhood, coupled with spiritual empowerment—more than methods, more than techniques, the self dominated and directed by the Holy Spirit.

The Lord requires clean hands and honest hearts for His work.

In isolating some of the elements that grant this enablement and comprise a responsible moral life for us, John Malchus Ellison accented these: sincerity, honesty, unselfishness, loyalty to principle, loyalty to truth, and integrity. He added, "These have no substitutes in the religious leader. The Lord requires clean hands and honest hearts for His work. He always did, He still does, He always will."

A church that has integrity usually grows out of the ministry of a minister who has integrity. It has become rather commonplace to hear some minister commonly referred to as a great leader, meaning that he or she mixes well with people and handles leadership responsibilities with adequacy, with timeliness, and with a strong sense of selfhood. Many ministers view this great-leader image as worthy of their concern and their effort. I hope this is not the dream you are dreaming—being a great leader. I hope you are not content to be viewed as a great leader. I hope your dream includes developing leaders by your leadership and trying to make your other leaders great. And this requires the work of teaching.

Jesus showed the way in this as in all other necessary areas. Concerned about the future of the work to which He set himself, He envisioned, selected, and trained a small group to expand and perpetuate His service as teacher, preacher, and healer. The demands upon Him had become unending and excessive, and aware that He had impacted a growing number of followers, He finally identified and isolated from within the larger crowd those who showed the most avid openness to Him and seemed reasonably gifted for what He would require of them.

According to Luke 6:12-13, when the time came for Jesus to single out those persons from the crowd and shape them for assignments under His direction, He withdrew to pray about the choices He must make. He prayed about it all throughout the night, exploring His options with God, with a God-illumined thought process. And the account tells us that when day came, "He called his disciples and chose twelve of them, whom he also named apostles" (Luke 6:13, NRSV).

The rest of the Gospels tell us the subsequent training of the Twelve. They underscore the time and the guidance Jesus gave in shaping them for leadership. He was sensible about the work God had assigned to His hands. He chose and developed others to assist Him in handling tasks that are required in each generation. The pastor must operate according to this vision already cast by our Lord.

SHARE YOUR DREAM OF VISIONARY LEADERS WHO POSSESS INTEGRITY

Let us highlight the ministry and not our own individual ministry—*the* ministry, meaning all of us working together as partners, in team fashion, and not working as competitive figures with our own private dream. We serve the whole Church a

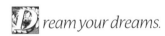 *ream your dreams.*

little at a time. Dream your dreams. Let them be big, but let them be the same dreams that our Lord had when He started the Church, to let it have integrity and to give His life for it.

It was a wise word that Roger Hazelton, former dean at Oberlin Graduate School of Theology, shared with his students. "The truly effective minister is not someone who can take oversight in the church but who can share insight with that church," he said. It is not one or the other; it is both. If we have insight, a church is more apt to give us and let us retain oversight. "Mark this," Hazelton said, "people in our churches today need more than strength for the mastery of life; they need light on the mystery of life, and there is a positive relationship between the two. In the last analysis, you cannot have the one without the other."

Develop great leaders. Pour your hearts into them. Do not

allow yourself to be the central focus. Be the figure around whom the congregation coalesces, but let them coalesce for the right reason—receiving truth shared from the heart that is concerned about them, so concerned that you spare no pain in order to help them have integrity.

Those who truly love the Lord and are deeply concerned to help people learn to live by God's will can develop churches with integrity because they will be contented, like that parson in Geoffrey Chaucer's *Canterbury Tales*, to gladly teach by following that teaching themselves.

❖3❖
HOW TO BE A CHRISTLIKE SERVANT LEADER
Adding Value and Serving Others
by John Maxwell

Since it is impossible to separate spiritual life and Christian leadership, personal spiritual health is an absolute essential for an effective church leader. In the church, potential leaders are totally disqualified if they are not godly persons with Christian disciplines in their lives. If Jesus were with us in human form, He would insist that Christian leadership starts and continues with the spirit of a servant enabled and enriched by the Spirit.

Henri Nouwen, in his powerfully insightful book *In the Name of Jesus,* underscores three real though subtle temptations every servant of Christ faces. Not surprisingly, these temptations are the same enticements Jesus faced as He began His earthly ministry.

The first temptation is to be self-sufficient. This temptation works directly against depending upon the Lord for strength, enablement, and guidance. This temptation prevents us from being vulnerable or becoming transparent. Self-sufficient leaders think and behave like they do not need others, but they do. How easy it is to forget the Kingdom principle "Without Me you can do nothing" (John 15:5, NKJV).

The second temptation is to be spectacular. It is what I call a celebrity mentality. Paul deliberately renounced this attitude. In Nouwen's words, "Jesus refused to be a stunt man. He did not come to walk on hot coals, swallow fire, or put His hand in a lion's mouth to demonstrate that He had something worthwhile to say." Regrettably, too many choose charisma over Christlikeness and slickness over spiritual authenticity.

The third temptation deals with a self-centered desire to be in charge, to control people, budgets, and churches. The church belongs to Christ, and He intends to be its head. Paul's comment is superb and humbling too: "We do not preach ourselves, but Je-

o say it simply,
one God is enough.

sus Christ as Lord, and ourselves as your servants for Jesus' sake" (2 Cor. 4:5). Giving in to this "be in charge" temptation can be seen in the life of so many people in Christian leadership positions who want to boss and lord it over others, to have their own way. To lead is necessary and useful, but to push, manipulate, and grasp for power—never. To say it simply, one God is enough.

The disciples suffered from a similar malady. Jesus had to guide them on a regular basis away from horizontal thinking to vertical thinking. Far too often they competitively compared themselves with one another. Too frequently they worried about getting credit or gaining prestige to feed their hungry egos. This grasping for standing shows clearly in the incident when James's and John's mother asked Jesus to give her boys places of honor in the Kingdom. Those sons must have been desperately hungry for position when they had to have their mom plead their case for a special place of prominence.

Jesus would have none of it and reminded them, "Whoever wants to become great among you must be your servant . . . just as the Son of Man did not come to be served, but to serve" (Matt. 20:26, 28). In the same passage, He said that such privilege "is not Mine to give, but it is for those for whom it is prepared by My Father" (v. 23, NKJV). Our Lord quickly turned them away from the horizontal to the vertical.

The prominence issue even reared its ugly head at the sacred supper in the Upper Room: "Within minutes they were bickering over who of them would end up the greatest. But Jesus intervened: 'Kings like to throw their weight around and people in authority like to give themselves fancy titles. It's not going to be that way with you. Let the senior among you become like the junior; let the leader act the part of the servant" (Luke 22:24-26, TM).

Every leader, whether ancient or modern, must face the reality that a genuinely satisfying life is focused more on giving than on getting. Though it is a difficult lesson to learn, serving always helps more people and brings greater satisfaction than grasping control. How Christian leaders can live out that reality and the joys they experience is explained in John 13, a magnificent mountain peak of Scripture. The passage offers wonderful deliverance and continual freedom from the three destructive temptations of self-sufficiency, celebrity mentality, and power addiction.

1. Christlike servants are motivated by love to serve others (vv. 1-2).

It was supper time. The devil had Judas Iscariot set for the betrayal. But even at that moment of deceitful treachery, Jesus' incredible love is the biblical pattern for servant leaders. Even at the time of painful betrayal, He showed His disciples an amazing threefold love. It was relational love: "He loved them to the end." His love was unconditional, so He continued to care deeply for Judas. He demonstrated an unselfish love, so at a time when He needed to be ministered to, He ministered to them. In His most difficult hour, Jesus became our example when He placed others before himself and when He loved them magnificently. What a pattern of love for leaders to follow!

The nonviolent civil rights leader Martin Luther King Jr. said it so well: "Everybody can be great because anybody can serve. You don't have to have a college degree to serve. You don't have to make your subject and verb agree to serve. You only need a heart full of grace. A soul generated by love."

Love is the essential foundation for every servant leader. Jesus underscores it with power in John 21 where He connects our love for Him with serving. In Jesus' first conversation with Peter following the disciple's denial, He asked, "Peter, do you love Me?" What a question to ask a guy who had hung around for three and a half years as your right-hand man and who was there during the trial. But Jesus asked the love question precisely because it was a critical personal issue with Peter. That is our issue too. Jesus asks, "Do you love Me?" It is the cornerstone—the backbone, the heart—of all Christian service and ministry.

2. Christlike servants possess a security that frees them to minister effectively (v. 3).

Insecurity always torpedoes leaders. But at this precise point there is amazing help available for a Christian leader.

Look at the verse closely and listen carefully for how it can empower your leadership. Jesus knew that the Father had put Him in control of everything. Our Lord knew who He was. He knew where He came from. He knew where He was going. He knew His position and did not flaunt it. He knew His calling and was faithful to it. And He knew His future and was willing to submit to it. Talk about being a secure person. That is a pattern worth following.

There is tremendous strength in security.

There is tremendous strength in security. As the disciples entered the Upper Room, the basin and the towel were pretty obvious. One devotional writer said, "Towels and basins are present in every relationship, but they are sometimes hard to recognize." Since the disciples were so insecure about who they were and what their position was, not one of them touched the basin.

I learned a long time ago that people who are secure do not have problems with titles, positions, offices, or nameplates. It is no big deal. *Leadership* magazine once sent their editors to interview me for a half a day on leadership. But at that time, I had no office. I had given it up because we had run out of space at INJOY. They were shocked. But why not? I believe the old saying is true: secure people do not have to fight for rights, titles, or positions.

I am always saddened when I see ministers trying so hard to gain positional leadership. They are not authentic leaders if they lead only by position. That is why I did a tape for the Injoy Life Club called *Leading from the Middle of the Pack*. To be a servant leader, you do not have to be at the top of the heap or have first place on an organizational chart. I know many leaders who lead from the middle of the pack. But only secure people can do that.

Security is an important requisite to great undertakings; only the secure will stretch. Security is also an important requisite for small undertakings; only the secure will stoop.

Christlike servanthood begins with security. The secure are into towels; the insecure are into titles. The secure are people-conscious; the insecure are position-conscious. The secure want to add value to others; the insecure want to receive value for themselves.

3. Christlike servants initiate ministries to others (vv. 4-5).

Jesus got up from the supper table and wrapped a towel around His waist. Then He poured water in a basin, washed the feet of the disciples, and dried them with the towel.

 *e washed their feet so they could see who they were.*

In that era, dirt and dust from the streets gathered on people's feet throughout the day. As one entered a home, he found a large pot of water with which he could wash his feet. In wealthy homes, however, servants washed guests' feet. On this occasion, the disciples did not volunteer to do the task because they did not want to look or feel inferior to one another. Jesus, however, put on a servant's uniform so all could see who He was. He washed their feet so they could see who they were.

I can tell you what they were thinking. Peter thinks, "Somebody will be washing feet, but not me because I know that I am not the least of the Twelve. I am part of the inner circle along with Jim and John. I am one of the big three." Go through the list and you can easily imagine the thoughts of the others. For example, Matt is probably thinking, "Since I am kind of an outsider, maybe I am the guy who ought to be doing this, but I do not want that job." Tom is probably thinking, "I doubt anybody is going to do this."

But in their presence, Jesus uses a towel and basin to transform the heart of Christian leadership forever. By this act of humility, He taught them and us the difference between Christ-centered leadership and secular leadership.

Here is how initiating service works even in contemporary life outside the church. After my nephew Troy earned a degree in business, I invited him to spend time with us in San Diego. So he did. Troy wanted to work in the financial world, and we had three men in the church who owned mortgage companies. He interviewed with them and he got a job.

Troy was really nervous the night before his first day at work. So we talked for a long time, and I suggested, "If you do these three things, you will be a vice president in the company by the time you are 30." He said, "What are they?" He had his legal pad out, ready to write.

I asked, "What time does work start tomorrow?"

Troy answered, "Eight o'clock."

I said, "Not for you. Never go in when anybody else goes in. Every morning go to work at 7:30."

Then I asked, "What time is lunch?"

He replied, "It is from 12 to 1."

I said, "Not for you. I encourage you to take about 30 minutes for lunch, and then get back to work."

Then I asked, "What time do you get off?"

Troy answered, "Five o'clock."

I said, "Not for you. You stay until 5:20 or 5:30 every day. Always work longer than anyone else."

Then I said, "Here is the second step: Every day do something for people around you that is not required of you. Do something beyond your job to add value to fellow workers. Within one month, every person in your department will say, 'Troy adds value to me; I get more accomplished because this guy is in my department.' They will not know how to handle you, but they will appreciate it."

Next I said, "Step number three: Ask for one 15-minute appointment with your boss. Walk into his office and say, 'I want you to know that when you hired me, you hired a person who will do anything within my power to make you successful. If you ever have any work that you do not know who to give it to, give it to me. I am here to make a difference for this company and for you.'"

Troy followed my suggestions. That first year he received two raises and two promotions. However, I was wrong in my prediction that he would become vice president by the time he was 30. It actually took him only three years.

It works the same way for church leaders. The secret is to initiate servant ministry to others. Blessing comes to us when we stop worrying about what we are going to get out of life, about rights, about degrees and start adding value and serving others.

While the disciples postured themselves to avoid serving, Jesus, for whom "the Father had put all things under his power" (John 13:2), initiated ministry to His followers. And He showed them and us how to do it.

4. Christlike servants receive ministry from others (vv. 6-7).

Peter and the others were doubtlessly surprised when Jesus took the basin and towel. They were slow learners about Kingdom principles. After being with our Lord for three years, and within sight of the Cross, they were about to eat their last meal together with the Master. Like us, competitive pride kept them from seeing clearly and hearing accurately the message of the Kingdom.

What the disciples did not learn
from His words, they were forced
to understand from His deeds.

Jesus took advantage of their self-seeking attitude to teach them an important Kingdom principle in a vivid, dramatic way—He became their servant. One little Sunday School student said after hearing this passage discussed, "Jesus sure shamed them, didn't He?"

What the disciples did not learn from His words, they were forced to understand from His deeds. The lesson for every leader in every setting is crystal clear—the servant is never greater than the master, and the authentic leader is servant of all.

In the foot washing, when Jesus got around to Peter, the big fisherman protested, "You're not going to wash my feet—ever!"

Jesus answered, "If I don't wash you, you can't be part of what I'm doing" (John 13:8, TM).

Peter agreed quickly when he understood the issues: "Master! . . . Not only my feet, then. Wash my hands! Wash my head!" (v. 9, TM).

The devoted New Testament scholar William Barclay in *The Gospel of John,* vol. 2 helps focus the significance of this encounter in one powerful sentence: "In every sphere of life this desire for prominence and this unwillingness to take a subordinate place wrecks the scheme of things." That is precisely why every authentic disciple of the Lord must give and receive ministry. Peter's humility grew like a spring flower when he understood that Jesus was teaching the two-sided dynamic of serving—it must be given and it must be received.

5. Christlike servants want nothing to interfere with their relationship with Jesus (vv. 8-9).

Servant leaders receive incredible strength from being closely connected to Christ. This dependence is easy to forget when people treat us like we are the last word on everything from religion to colors for the new sanctuary drapes. But we are nothing without Christ.

So while Peter felt incredibly unworthy to have his feet washed by Jesus, he knew he needed and wanted a tight relationship with Christ. So when Jesus says, "Unless I wash you, you have no part with me," Peter gladly gave up his resistance: "Feet, hands, head—everything. So I may be close to you and have part in the significant things you are doing."

Any price of humility, any acceptance of what we do not understand, and any confusion about serving is worthwhile if it keeps us near the Lord. Always keep this warning before you: Churches cannot be what God intends them to be without a leader who keeps close to Christ. Without such an authentic personal relationship to Christ in us, the churches we lead become counterfeit, empty, and secularized.

6. Christlike servants teach servanthood by their example (vv. 12-17).

No guesswork or complicated exegesis here. Having finished the foot washing, Jesus asks an incredibly instructive question: "Do you understand what I have done for you?" (John 13:12). Then before they could answer a single word, He says, "I have set you an example that you should do as I have done. I tell you the truth; no servant is greater than his master, nor is a messenger greater than the one who sent him" (vv. 15-16).

Read carefully to fully comprehend what Jesus was saying: "Now that you know these things, you will be blessed if you do them" (v. 17). I appreciate the way *The Message* puts verse 17: "If you understand what I'm telling you, act like it—and live a blessed life." What an example. What a promise. What a commission. What a mountain peak of instruction and inspiration. What an affirmation for Christlike servants.

ake up the towel.
Pick up a trowel.

Jesus shows us that teaching servant leadership to others is done most effectively by serving others. Serving another in the name of our Lord is a more effective way to teach and inspire than a thousand pronouncements or 500 sermons on the subject. Take up the towel. Pick up a trowel. Grab a hammer. Wash the dishes. Dial the phone. Pull the weeds. Or donate blood. Then notice how much more attentively people listen to your preaching and teaching. Watch how they follow your example of serving. Real leaders follow a West Pointer's wonderful advice: "Make sure the troops are settled and fed before you take care of your own needs."

7. Christlike servants live a blessed life (vv. 16-17).

Albert Schweitzer—missionary, musician, and religious humanitarian—knew and lived out this idea in the daily events of his ministry. Based on his unselfish service and satisfying achievements, Schweitzer said, "I don't know what your destiny will be, but one thing I know: the only ones among you who will be really happy are those who will have sought and found how to serve." He learned that lesson from our Lord.

When Jesus saw His ministry drawing huge crowds, He climbed a hillside. He wanted the disciples and interested persons in the crowd to have an accurate understanding of the blessed life. To those He was shaping into leaders He taught:

You're blessed when you're at the end of your rope. With less of you there is more of God and his rule.

You're blessed when you feel you've lost what is most dear to you. Only then can you be embraced by the One most dear to you.

You're blessed when you're content with just who you

are—no more, no less. That's the moment you find yourselves proud owners of everything that can't be bought.

You're blessed when you've worked up a good appetite
for God. He's food and drink in the best meal you'll ever eat.

You're blessed when you care. At the moment of being
"care-full," you find yourselves cared for.

You're blessed when you get your inside world—your
mind and heart—put right. Then you can see God in the
outside world.

You're blessed when you can show people how to co-
operate instead of compete or fight. That's when you discover who you really are, and your place in God's family.

You're blessed when your commitment to God pro-
vokes persecution. The persecution drives you even deeper
into God's kingdom *(Matt. 5:3-10, TM)*.

The Beatitudes express most profoundly and practically the
fundamental disciplines of Christian servanthood and the amazing satisfactions of the inner life.

8. Christlike servants live their lives in opposition to the philosophy of the world (vv. 18-19).

The message of these verses paints a painful picture of the
betrayal. This passage helps us see how two different value sys-
tems are at work at the same time in the world. Let's get it crystal
clear—every church leader is constantly in danger of being in-
fected by the anti-Kingdom viruses that are so prevalent in our
secular society. The spirit of the world almost chokes us at times.
Possessions, power, prestige, and one-upmanship are its symptoms. Our preventive vaccines and healing antibiotics are Scripture, prayer, fellowship, and contact with Christ.

A. W. Tozer, the spiritual giant from an earlier era, said it
well: "The Christian is an odd number anyway. He feels supreme
love for one he has never seen; talks familiarly every day to someone he cannot see; expects to go to heaven on the virtue of another; empties himself in order to be full; admits he is wrong so that
he can be declared right; goes down in order to get up; is strongest
when he is weakest; richest when he is poorest; happiest when he
feels the worst; he dies so that he can live; forsakes in order to
have; gives away so he can keep; sees the invisible, hears the in-

audible; and knows that which passes understanding." No wonder the world considers us strange. Without apology, we serve another Master, have a different mission, and live by different values.

> *o wonder our leadership style*
> *must be so different from*
> *Main Street or Wall Street.*

Paul advises us, "Don't push your way to the front; don't sweet-talk your way to the top. Put yourself aside, and help others get ahead. Don't be obsessed with getting your own advantage. Forget yourselves long enough to lend a helping hand" (Phil. 2:3-4, TM). Such a way of doing service is in serious conflict with the philosophy of the world and its secular values. No wonder our leadership style must be so different from Main Street or Wall Street.

9. The Christlike servant brings Jesus to others (v. 20).

Jesus said, "Make sure you get this right: Receiving someone I send is the same as receiving me, just as receiving me is the same as receiving the One who sent me" (v. 20, TM).

Mother Teresa made the world spiritually curious by living out the Christlike servant style to India. An American tourist, as he observed Mother Teresa dressing a dying leper's wounds, asked permission to take a photograph. Then, after seeing firsthand the tenderness with which the saintly nun dressed the gaping hole where the leper's nose once was, the American spoke with mingled awe and repulsion, "Sister, I would not do what you are doing for a million dollars!"

Mother Teresa replied, "Neither would I, my friend. Neither would I for a million, but I gladly do it for Jesus."

Bringing Jesus to others causes us to live out several biblical paradoxes. Think about the wonderful mystery of it all as shown in this list:

If I want to save my life, I must lose my life (Luke 9:24-26). If I want to be lifted up, I must humble myself (James 4:10). If I want to be first, I must be last (Matt. 20:16). If I want to rule, I must serve (Luke 22:26-27). If I want to live, I must put to death the deeds of the body (Rom. 8:13). If I want to be strong, I must be weak (2 Cor. 12:10). If I want to inherit the Kingdom, I must be poor in spirit (Matt. 5:3). If I want to reproduce, I must die (John 12:24).

NO PLACE TOO SMALL FOR MY BEST

Somewhere I discovered this poem. It has a message God wants every leader to put into practice:

Little Places
"Father, where shall I work today?"
And my love flowed warm and free.
He pointed out a tiny spot and said,
"Tend that place for me."
I answered Him quickly, "Oh, no! Not that!
Why, no one would ever see,
No matter how well my work was done;
not that little place for me!"
The word He spoke, then, wasn't stern
He answered me tenderly:
"Nazareth was a little place,
and so was Galilee."

For everyone who seeks to be a Christ-centered servant leader, I challenge you to consider this list of *whatevers* by which I try to shape my life of service in Christ's kingdom:

(1) Whatever I do, I want to *honor God.* (2) Whatever I do, I want to do it with *all my heart.* (3) Whatever I do, I want to do it with *others.* (4) Whatever I do, I want to *honor and add value* to others.

Revisit your call to ministry. Refurbish your inner world with the beauty of Christlikeness.

Revisit your call to ministry. Refurbish your inner world with the beauty of Christlikeness. Reinvent your leadership strategies around the Christ-centered servant model. That is an adventuresome pathway to bringing people to new life in Christ, to producing new Kingdom accomplishments, and to finding new joy in service.

The higher your status or standing in a Kingdom assignment, organization, or local congregation, the harder it is to remember that you are always a servant to the people of God and that Jesus is Lord and Master. Titles, authority, being boss, controlling budgets, and perks must always be used under the ultimate Lordship of Jesus.

Your congregation does not belong to you; it belongs to Jesus. You do not own your ministry; it belongs to your Master. Your church staff is not "my staff" and not "my people." And the congregation is not "my members." You are merely a steward entrusted by the Head of the Church with an assignment, and faithfulness is required of stewards. To forget this fact for even a moment is to open the door of your heart to sinful self-sovereignty, selfish bulldog stubbornness, and administrative shipwreck.

Hear again these energizing words from Jesus directed to Christlike servant leaders in every age: "Make sure you get this right: Receiving someone I send is the same as receiving me, just as receiving me is the same as receiving the One who sent me" (John 13:20, TM).

· 4 ·

SEVEN HABITS OF A VISIONARY LEADER

Developing the Heart of a Champion Pastor for the 21st Century

by Dale Galloway

A leader must know the Leader—Jesus Christ—and follow Him. This is the No. 1 difference between secular and spiritual leadership.

God only uses a person in a leadership assignment to the degree that person is submitted to the Lordship of Christ. The genuineness of this Godward relationship makes believing people willing to follow us and at the same time makes us worthy of being followed.

Paul encouraged Timothy to aspire to become a church leader when he advised his son in ministry, "If anyone sets his heart on being an overseer, he desires a noble task" (1 Tim. 3:1). That sentence sure sounds like wholehearted encouragement and authentic reassurance for anyone who wants to lead in the church.

But in our inner world—the place known only to God and us—let's be seriously sobered by the fact that in Timothy's time, leadership offered few privileges and little prestige. In those days, Christian leadership brought nagging frustrations and demanded life-threatening sacrifices. Then—as seen in the ministry of Jesus, Paul, and Stephen—leaders often experienced hardship, contempt, rejection, and even death. Being a leader in the Early Church was risky, thankless, and terrifying.

However, in spite of the difficulties and demands, it is plain the church has always needed more and better leaders. I believe

Paul had the church's best interest in mind when he encouraged Timothy to become a leader. The church was to benefit from Timothy's ministry. Contemporary leaders and would-be leaders need to clearly see this reality. An opportunity of leadership in the church is not for a leader's personal benefit, but for the good of the Body of Christ.

According to Paul, those who aspire to be leaders have a worthy goal, but the ambition must be for the church's good and strengthening. J. Oswald Chambers in *Spiritual Leadership* helps us balance personal ambition and authentic usefulness in service with this insightful sentence: "An ambition that has as its center the glory of God and the welfare of His church is not only legitimate, but it is also positively praise-worthy."

WHY DO YOU WANT TO LEAD?

For every leader, a fundamental, soul-searching question must be answered in his or her heart: Why do I want to lead?

*Human leaders must lead
to please the Leader.*

The real motivation must be for one's life and service to make a significant impact for Christ. Christian leaders must aspire to multiply and maximize the results of their service by accomplishing more through leading others than they could ever accomplish by themselves. Authentic Kingdom leaders, more than anything else, must desire a satisfying life of service filled with optimum usefulness to the cause of Christ. Human leaders must lead to please the Leader.

In thinking clearly about our motives for leading, a basic test is asking yourself how willing you are to follow. No one leads effectively for long who does not also follow. The call is to follow Jesus as well as to follow other leaders in the work of God. Real leaders follow as well as lead; often both following and leading are done at the same time.

Another part of the puzzle must also be considered. No one can lead who has no followers. Management expert Peter Drucker explains this need in seven short words: "A leader is someone who has followers." This means that even though an individual may be officially elected to an assignment or appointed to a role of leadership, he or she does not actually lead until someone follows. An accurate proverb explains why: "He who thinks he is the leader and has no followers is only taking a walk."

The way a visionary leader gains followers is by calling people to Kingdom causes that have worthy goals and eternal results built into them. Concerning this calling to noble causes, Bob Briner and Ray Pritchard in *The Leadership Lessons of Jesus* advise us, "When you feel called to lead, and when you discover someone you really want and need to be involved in your endeavor, don't be coy. Follow the example of Jesus and *ask* them to join you. People want to be asked and feel needed."

An additional factor must also be faced. Followers are more likely to follow the leader who demonstrates character, integrity, and authenticity because no one wants to follow a charlatan or impostor, especially in church.

ARE LEADERS BORN OR DEVELOPED?

I confess I have not always been sure how to answer this question. I wrestled day and night for weeks with this issue while God was shaping my decision to accept Asbury Seminary's invitation to establish the Beeson Leadership Center.

Thomas Carlyle's *Theory of History* says that some individuals are destined to be leaders before they were born. That means, of course, that you can never become a leader unless you were destined to be one. Such a belief leaves many Christian pastors shut out of any ministry that requires leadership.

On the growing leadership side of this debate, I went back to a book authored by my early mentor, Dr. Harold Reed, long-term president of Olivet Nazarene University. In his book on leadership, Reed insists that leaders are made, developed, and grown. He illustrates the point with convincing examples. His leadership development strategy moved forward on three levels simultaneously. While developing a great educational institution, he developed himself into an effective leader and built strong leaders around him. His three-level pattern also works effectively in the church—build a great church, improve yourself, and at the same time develop those around you.

VISIONARY LEADERS DO THE RIGHT THINGS
FOR THE RIGHT REASONS

In my struggle over this endowed or developed leadership issue, I went back to study Drucker's influential book *The Effective Executive.* There he makes a strong case for developing leaders in one
short sentence: "I've not come across a single natural executive who
was born effective." In that same volume, Drucker also advises that
anyone who wants to lead should not worry about doing everything
perfectly but commit to doing the right things for the right reasons
every time. That includes development of oneself and others. Consider his idea carefully with me—isn't that exactly what the cause of
Christ needs from effective human leaders in every setting?

Force yourself to question any messianic notions that you
have all the answers. Keep reminding yourself that being in a
leadership slot does not make you able to think better than others in and outside your organization. Almost everyone you meet
can help you discover at least a part of the right answers to your
situation, providing you are willing to ask and listen. Nonpro-
ductive leaders are usually people who know it all or who are
too insecure to ask others for their input.

> *Force yourself to question
> any messianic notions that
> you have all the answers.*

As you consider input from a variety of sources, you will
uncover viable principles to shape effective strategies. When
such winning strategies are developed, Drucker advises they
should be done over and over and over and over again. That advice worked especially well in Portland when we were developing our small-group ministry. That is the reason group ministry
flourished until we had 5,000 attending each week. The secret:
we kept doing what brought desired results.

In looking back over my ministry journey, I feel like I stand
on my father's shoulders. He specialized in doing the right things
over and over. Dad, who served for over 30 years as a Nazarene
district superintendent, provided me with a tremendous foundation for visionary leadership that I frequently draw on to this

day. When I was growing up, Nazarene denominational leaders often stayed as overnight guests in our home. In those days before motels became so common, church leaders stayed at our house so often that a guest bedroom was called the general superintendent's room. We enjoyed fellowship with a constant flow of missionaries, district leaders, evangelists, and key laymen who stayed overnight at our place.

I heard many ideas as a kid that shaped my ways of doing ministry. Though I was not aware of their impact at the time, I learned a lot about leadership just by listening. To this day, strategies and solutions sometimes come into my mind almost automatically because of what I overheard as a child. As I look back over three generations of ministers in my family—my grandfather, my father, and me—I realize how important it is to keep doing the right things for the right reasons over and over.

From my experiences at Portland, my ministerial training, keeping close to ministry peers, and what I assimilated in my childhood home, I have formulated seven habits for effective church leaders. These habits have shaped my ministry and continue to guide my thinking even now. These habits have also been affirmed over and over by the incredible influence of many of my admired mentors like my dad, Dr. Harold Reed, and Dr. Robert Schuller.

HABIT 1—HAVE A CLEAR VISION

No pastor can effectively lead others until he or she knows where to go. This essential law of ministry is fully as reliable as the law of gravity in the physical universe. A nowhere destination always results from a nowhere plan.

Asbury graduate Tim Barton defines vision in this inspiring, insightful way: "Vision addresses the future by creating a picture of what we desire tomorrow to look like. Vision is a destination toward a tomorrow that will be better, more successful, or more desirable than what is real at the present moment. Vision is a signpost that supplies direction and guidance, a target at which the organization aims. . . . Vision is more than just a mental image of the future. But within that image lies the energy and passion to inspire one to make it happen." Vision sees a better, more desirable future and provides direction and fuels motivation for its achievement. The probing question for shaping such a vision is: Where do you see your church 5 years from now, 10 years from now, 20 years from now?

• **Start by developing a long view.** When I went to visit Dr. Cho's church in Seoul, Korea, I stayed on the 16th floor of a large downtown hotel. To reach my room, I used an elevator marked to go as high as the 18th floor. From my room I admired a beautiful, expansive view of the city. On the last morning of my visit, however, I was invited with a group to have breakfast with Dr. Cho and was told we would meet on the 36th floor. "I thought this hotel had only 18 floors," I said in astonishment.

*o clarify your vision, figure out
ways to take yourself to the
36th floor of your situation.*

But to get to the 36th floor, I had to go around a corner from the elevators I had been using. Though I enjoyed my 16th-floor view, it did not compare with the 36th-floor view. I could see so much more from there—my perspective of Seoul was incredibly improved by going 20 floors higher.

Every spiritual leader who wants to accomplish significant achievement for God has to have 36th-floor experiences so he or she sees clearer, further, and more than anyone else. To clarify your vision, figure out ways to take yourself to the 36th floor of your situation. The experience will lift your sights, clarify your vision, refocus your perspective, and energize your faith.

• **Communication increases commitment.** For more than 10 years, I led seminars on small-group ministry across America where I met pastors and laypeople from all types and sizes of churches. At break times, laypeople often said to me, "Could you get our pastor to have a little more vision? We could do something significant for God if our leader had a bigger vision."

Right after that, a pastor would walk up, sometimes from the same church, and ask, "Do you think you could get our laypeople to see a larger vision? Then we could do something at our church."

The problem is often poor communication. Sadly, in many churches, lay leaders are headed one way while their pastor is going another way. If they could come together to discover and to communicate God's vision for their church, they would have incredible strength. Unity of purpose flows from a shared vision that is communicated clearly and frequently. Share the vision often. Talk it up in committees, from the pulpit, and in private conversations. There is magnetic power in a unified vision that every person on the team understands and works to achieve.

• **Vision makes church appealing.** One Sunday, a pastor I heard about asked church board members to come forward for prayer. He noticed a man whom he had not seen before come to the front of the church. To keep from embarrassing the newcomer, the pastor whispered to the stranger, "This is only for the board."

The man answered with intense sincerity, "If anyone in this place is more bored than me, I'd like to meet them."

Sadly, many churches are full of bored people. Regrettably, many of them have never known anything else at church. I wonder why they keep coming. When visiting a church, you can tell in a few minutes if a congregation has a shared vision. When they share a vision for their future, excitement and anticipation can be felt everywhere. Those churches have a future, and they are on their way to achieving it.

• **Vision takes a church beyond maintenance.** In church, everything is energized with a vision. Consequently, when a church shares a great vision from God, it thrives rather than survives. Then a church no longer merely exists in a maintenance mode; it has an inspiring dream that motivates an enabling passion to reach the lost. Becoming fishers of men is Jesus' promise for His Church—surely that means more than spending years listening to lifeless lectures about fish or taking graduate courses in oceanography.

How to Turn a Vision into Reality

But how can a vision be turned into reality? Here are several ways to do it.

• **You must picture the vision.** Everyone possesses some ability to visualize but needs to be encouraged to use that ability. All of us visualized dreams as children and continue to do so in some areas of our existence throughout life. The mighty God, who communicates through the Holy Spirit, wants you as a visionary leader to see a picture of the church He wants to create through you in your setting.

• **Give your heart to the vision.** Become really passionate, intense, and consumed by your vision. One old-time pastor used to say, "Nobody thinks a pastor is serious about anything until he seems half-crazy over it." I think he has a valid point worthy of our consideration.

I started my first church in Grove City, Ohio, in 1963 by going door to door. More than anything I wanted to reach people for Christ. You might call it knee-knocking evangelism because as I knocked on a door, my knees knocked so much that I hoped no one would answer.

> *Door to door—that was the way I gave heart and energy and life to my vision.*

Door to door—that was the way I gave heart and energy and life to my vision. I did not know how to personally lead a person to Christ. The older ministers I asked did not know how. The young beginners didn't have a clue. But winning new people became such a passion for me that I prayed every day about it. I asked every pastor I'd meet, "How do you do this?"

Then one day, as this burning earnestness was being turned into a consuming passion, God brought me in touch with Gordon Walker of Campus Crusade for Christ at Ohio State University. As Gordon and I sat together in the Student Union, he showed me in five minutes how to do personal evangelism—in one, two, three steps. He wrote the formula and steps on a paper napkin that I put in my pocket.

A short while later when a lady answered my knock at her door, I asked if she had heard about the four spiritual laws. She answered, "What's that?" Then she invited me into her house to talk about the Lord. I took the napkin out, laid it on the table, and went through the steps Gordon taught me. Then I asked her if she would like to pray and receive Christ. She replied, "I'd love to, but I don't know how."

So I prayed the prayer Gordon Walker had written on the napkin and the lady received Christ.

Personal evangelism started to work at Grove City when it became my passion. When I was back at that church many years later, I renewed acquaintances with 25 individuals that I led to Christ because of my soul-winning passion in those earlier years.

Personal evangelism was a new paradigm for me then. But for the vision to impact people and turn them to Christ, it had to become a burning desire of my life before it touched anyone else.

• **Make sure your vision pleases God.** Test your vision against Scripture. Pray over it. Talk it over with people of faith.

We must pray until we know God is pleased with the vision. We have to consider all the issues from His perspective. We must evaluate every alternative until we know this is what God wants us to do in this place at this time. Guidance is promised in the Bible. Seek it. Follow it. Trust it.

• **Get focused.** Concentrate on the vision and focus your dream on your particular assignment. For example, winning people is important for every church, but some congregations live in a spiritual never-never land where winning people is frequently discussed but no specific plans are ever developed.

It is easy to miss turning our vision into a reality by giving attention to too many things. Then a church's vision gets fragmented and diffused. This happens when many persons in a congregation have ideas about what a church is supposed to do and be. A clear focus helps prevent such a problem. A defining vision tells everyone what you will do and rules out everything else. A clearly understood vision focuses a congregation on its reason for being.

• **Organize to accomplish your vision.** Leadership is not doing the work of 10 people but getting 10 people to do the work of 10 people. Neh. 3 provides us a powerful example of organizing people, dividing huge work loads into smaller tasks. It provides a helpful pattern for involving, mobilizing, and getting everyone to do something important to help accomplish the vision.

Authentic leaders help every believer find ways to become useful. And visionary leadership provides a satisfying way for each person to become involved in fulfilling the dream.

• **Risk failure.** No one accomplishes anything great in a church without taking risks. Achieving a worthwhile vision always demands daring and adventurous faith.

This does not mean jumping off tall buildings or doing something stupid or suicidal. What I mean to suggest here is more like climbing stairsteps, so as you achieve one step of your vision, you then stretch to reach the next step. To be firmly convinced, revisit the ministries of Jesus, Paul, and the greats of Church history.

Let's admit that most human beings, including us, are more comfortable being settlers than pioneers. A sad example comes from an early settlement on the North American shores when a town council was asked to build two miles of roads into the wilderness. They voted no because they feared the risks of the

> et's admit that most human beings,
> including us, are more comfortable
> being settlers than pioneers.

wilds. Think about that—pioneer people who had risked crossing an ocean to find freedom were now afraid of two miles in the wilderness. Sadly, we are sometimes like that. Visionary leadership, however, understands that most advances in Christian history happened when someone took risks—often incredibly dangerous risks.

• **Put faith into action.** Achieving faith means putting concepts into work clothes, conversations into Christ-centered action, and ideas into actual ministry. Faith is more than concept, hope, or theory—it is action. Long before New Hope Community had a singles ministry, our staff dreamed and prayed about serving the large single population in Portland. We talked about it. We brainstormed. We conducted feasibility studies. We learned all we could about singles ministry by studying both successful and ailing programs in other churches. A long time before we started, we envisioned what could be. As the years passed, our singles ministry developed to the point that we often had as many as 900 people attending. Why? Because we put our faith and effort into achieving our vision.

HABIT 2—INFLUENCE INFLUENCERS

When I graduated from seminary, I wanted to be called Rev. Dale Galloway. Before long, however, I learned leadership is not in titles but in influence. A leader must earn influence before he or she can influence influencers.

But how does any church leader—clergy or laity—gain influence? You cannot buy it or force it. Instead, you have to earn it. No matter how great your vision is or how gifted you may be, you cannot fulfill a God-sized calling without influencing influencers.

Someone has said that leadership is influence. The greatest kind of leadership is being able to influence those who in turn influence everyone else. It is important for every pastor to learn how to expand his or her leadership in this way.

Gaining and maintaining influence has to do with recognizing and utilizing your basic leadership inclinations and strengths. Years ago, a sociologist taught me about two distinct kinds of leaders. And I never forgot what I learned because it was such a key factor in my years at Portland.

Task Leaders or Cohesive Leaders

First, there is the cohesive leader who creates togetherness and warm, fuzzy relationships. These people are highly relational.

Then there is the task leader. He or she has visions, sets goals, and goes all out to accomplish the dream. The task leader makes a congregation believe that the task will be accomplished somehow.

Woody Hayes, former football coach at Ohio State, was a task leader who was always determined to win, no matter what. His coaching record shows how much he achieved. An interesting story about Hayes reports how he went to Ohio State stadium when he was an old man. As the story goes, there was a parking place but it was not big enough to allow him to park and still open his car door. To complicate matters even more, the space was uphill. So Woody solved the problem by pushing his car uphill into the spot. He had been a task leader so long that he determined to make the situation work somehow. And he did.

If you are a task leader, you need to try to be more cohesive. If you are cohesive, you need to become more task-focused. I am fortunate that my wife is a cohesive person-focused leader. As a result, when people were upset with me, they would call my wife. She softened the sharp edges my task qualities sometimes created.

Sometimes my wife would say, "Dale, slow down. People want to go with you, but they don't understand yet."

I replied, "I've said it six times. What more do they want?"

"Well, slow up. Wait. They want to go with you, but they don't understand it yet." At our house we often laugh about all that. Now after these years, Margi is becoming more task-oriented and I am becoming more cohesive-oriented.

Which kind of leadership does your church most need?

Which kind of leadership does your church most need? Both cohesive and task leaders are needed. My father, who supervised many congregations in northern Ohio, had responsibility for calling several pastors across the years to a church that had a strong lay task-leader. Whenever Dad sent a task pastor there, strong lay leader and task pastor would lock horns—sometimes it seemed like they might kill each other. Then the pastor would be pressured to leave—and the departing ministers were usually glad to have this strong lay leader out of their lives. Next pastor, gone. Next pastor, gone. About every two years, that congregation was forced to call a new pastor.

Finally, Dad found a man who was so cohesive and loving that he had a good word to say about everyone. In a few months, the lay leader and the pastor became close friends because their strengths complemented each other. As a result, that church enjoyed a long and fruitful ministry from their cohesive pastor over many years. That was possible because the congregation had both a cohesive leader and a task leader who naturally worked together well.

As an irresistible point of operations, a pastor needs to understand when it is time to be more task-focused and when to be more cohesive.

Of course, there will be ebbs and flows in church life where one quality is needed more than the other. Beyond those cycles, however, two things are always needed: (1) Work at expanding your own leadership characteristics; (2) Identify influencers based on those who are cohesive leaders and those who are task leaders. Value both task and cohesive influencers—pastors generally appreciate only one or the other.

How Do Influencers Get Their Influence?

A clergy or lay leader gains influence in many ways. To aid my memory, I use six **C**s when I think about where influence comes from. Notice how positive and useful these sources are to the well-being of a church:

- Clear vision—As Elmer Towns says, "When people buy your dream they buy into your leadership."
- Credibility—You gain credibility by doing what you say you will do.
- Confidence—Influencing others is hard without being a faith-filled and hope-filled person.
- Character—Your actions and attitudes speak as loudly, if not more loudly, than your words; you have to model ministry to teach ministry.
- Commitment—As a leader, you must be the most committed of all; people will not follow you far unless you are deeply committed to your vision.
- Courage—Faith involves taking risks; you do not hit home runs unless you are willing to strike out.

When this list is considered fully, it is obvious that influencers are among the most gifted and most faithful people in any church. They are the people who help a pastor accomplish the vision.

How to Work Through Influencers

Every church has a power structure, even though we sometimes ignore or deny it. Often the most influential persons in a congregation are not members of official boards or committees. Nevertheless, in order to achieve the vision, every pastor must

very church has a power structure, even though we sometimes ignore or deny it.

identify the influencers, understand what gives them influence, and purposefully work with them. Oftentimes influencers are the most dedicated, well-respected members of the congregation.

In a church of 100, there may be about 5 individuals who influence the entire congregation. Though the interpersonal dynamics may be significantly different in larger churches, influencers still affect how a church functions, and they have amazing organizational power. For example, when New Hope Community Church topped 6,000 in attendance, no 1 layperson any longer had influence across the entire congregation. There were, however, several persons who had incredible influence on smaller, select segments of the congregation. Sometimes pastors of larger churches tend to overlook this dynamic.

Be aware also that some people on every church board or committee always watch to see how the influencers think about an issue. They then vote with the influencer. That means an influencer generally controls more than his own vote on an issue. It is amazing to watch how this interaction works in decision groups.

Influencers, if you ask them, can help you with answers to several important questions like: What is the history of this church? What were the struggles of this congregation to get where it is? To really lead effectively, you must understand the meaning of these stories. Learn the priorities influencers have. Identify their concerns. Listen closely to what they tell you about themselves and others. It also helps to listen for what they leave out in their stories. Listen especially carefully for what they tell you about former pastors and previous staff members.

If you ignore influencers or, in the name of fair-mindedness, try treating them like everyone else, you will never lead a church to the fulfillment of its potential. You may have lofty vision and divinely directed goals, but if you cannot or will not influence these key people, you will not be able to accomplish great achievements.

Let's think of specific, useful ways to effectively influence influencers.

1. Spend time with individual influencers.
2. Be interested in them as individuals.
3. Listen to them so you can better understand them.
4. Respect and value them.
5. Share your vision and goals with them personally.
6. Take time to explain where you are going.
7. Let them know your heart.
8. Enlist their help; be enthusiastic in acknowledging that you cannot accomplish your goals alone.

9. Plant seeds and allow time for harvest.

10. Keep constantly in touch with them.

Don't be naive concerning influential people. Just as money, spiritual vitality, and relational contacts are needed to lead a church, the support of influencers must be continually and purposefully cultivated.

A Lesson from a Parking Lot

Let me explain how influencing influencers worked on a project at New Hope Community Church. Exploding growth took place soon after we moved into our multipurpose building. Having three services and sustaining attendance depended on keeping everything on a tight schedule. If we didn't keep things moving on time, the parking lots jammed, and to avoid traffic congestion, people would drive away.

I began to observe an attendance pattern. One Sunday people would be seated clear to the wall, and the next week there would be five empty rows at the back—it was an ebb and flow. I asked myself, *What's happening?* I asked ushers and staff members about the problem. The solution was simple but expensive—there was not enough blacktop parking. In rainy Oregon, empty fields for parking do not work because it becomes too muddy. So I said to the board, "We've got a problem; we need to build more parking lots."

The members started to overreact and grouse like every church board does at times: "Oh, we can't afford more parking. Pastor, you know, we've got this big debt. And the timing is not right." On and on it went. I suggested we table the idea.

Later, during the month, I went to see Tom. We had lunch. In our conversation I simply said, "Tom, you know God has called us to reach the unchurched of Portland, but people are driving off every Sunday because they cannot find parking places. We can't have that, can we?"

Tom replied, "No, Pastor, we can't have that." That was about all that was said.

Then I went out to lunch with another man. Then another. All three were influencers on the official board. I was doing influencing homework—a vital component in making good decisions.

Next board meeting, I asked, "Any old business we need to discuss?"

Tom spoke up, "Yeah, we need to build that parking lot."

"I second it," influencer number two said.

Then to strengthen support, influencer number three added, "I third it."

was doing influencing homework—a vital component in making good decisions.

It took one minute. No discussion. The board voted unanimously to build a parking lot.

Then in front of the group I said, "Tom, that was a great idea you had to build that parking lot. I'm really proud of your leadership." He smiled a knowing smile. See how it works.

Influencing influencers is not devious manipulation but an essential dynamic in organizational life. It is one of the significant ways decision-making groups work.

HABIT 3—BUILD A WINNING TEAM

Everyone accomplishes more when working as a team. The word *synergism* captures the idea. Synergism simply means everyone combines his or her unique giftedness to produce significant achievement for Christ. The apostle Paul explained that even though every person is a separate part of the Body of Christ, effectiveness is vastly multiplied when each part does its work in cooperation with all the other parts.

Though I am not an equestrian specialist, I have been told one horse can pull 2 tons by itself. That means two horses working separately will be able to pull 4 tons, 2 tons per horse. But when two horses are teamed together, they can pull 18 tons. Apparently this fact of synergism is why Scripture has so much to say about spiritual gifts and about how we need each other in our efforts to build the Kingdom.

Leadership Paradigms Have Changed

For building solidly efficient teams in a congregation, it is absolutely crucial that we understand how leadership paradigms have radically changed in recent years. The former top-down way of working, where the pastor is boss and everyone follows his or her orders, does not work anymore. That's out—hierarchal dictatorship is not effective in corporate settings, nor does it work in church.

isionary leaders must build individuals together into teams and empower them for their ministry.

Visionary leaders must build individuals together into teams and empower them for their ministry. It takes delegation, motivation, patience, and an abiding confidence that teams work better than lone rangers. I love to think about the positive implications of Elton Trueblood's wise words in *Your Other Vocation,* "If the average church should suddenly take seriously the notion that every laymember—man or woman—is really a minister of Christ, we could have something like a revolution in a very short time."

Last year I was invited to consult with the Cincinnati Vineyard Church. They have 7 services over each weekend, so they have 3,500 attending every weekend in a building that seats 500. They maximized everything. I will never forget a staff meeting where they put about 125 different ministries on the table for discussion. As we talked, they told me this one is done by this staff person, this by a volunteer, and this is by a lay pastor.

You know what most of the discussion was about that day? They were trying to sort out who they would call pastor. It was such an inspiring and wonderfully confusing scene of ministry. As I left, I said to myself, "How different from how most of us do church."

Laity Want to Be in the Action

As laypersons are mobilized for significant service, they start to function as a ministry team working together to produce incredible results. When real teamwork happens, the gap between what clergy does and what laity does closes. Surprisingly, the process snowballs, so as you build teams, lay leaders will find ways to build teams under them, and the results are multiplied over and over again.

An important slant for a pastor to realize is that potential lay leaders are no longer satisfied to serve as mere greeters, ushers, parking supervisors, or offering counters. They want to do life-changing ministry like winning people, teaching the Bible, hands-on compassionate ministry, and crisis pastoral care. I delight to recall that Early Church record when Stephen and Philip signed on to serve tables but soon found themselves squarely in the middle of the life-and-death action. Stephen became the first Christian martyr. Philip opened the gospel to the Samaritans and Africans. I believe with all my heart that God has many contemporary surprises for the lay leaders you develop in your church.

Our need to develop a team reminds me of a modern parable. The traveling salesman hit a slick spot with his car and slid into a ditch. So he went to a nearby farmer's house. The farmer hitched up his mule to pull the car out of the ditch.

Then he shouted, "Pull, John." Nothing happened.

"Pull, Tom." Nothing happened.

Then, "Pull, Elmo." And the mule easily pulled the car back up onto the road.

The amazed salesman asked the farmer, "Why didn't you call his name in the first place?"

The farmer answered with earthy wisdom, "Elmo doesn't work unless he thinks he's on a team." People are like that too—they always work better on a team.

Lessons from Dayton

A few months ago, Michael Slaughter of Ginghamsburg United Methodist Church near Dayton asked me to preach in his four services on the weekend. What a team ministry he has going.

About Tuesday, I got a phone call informing me they were meeting as a staff and needed my exact outline for my sermon for the following Sunday. Fortunately, I had it finished, so I went through it point by point on the phone with them. Then I faxed the outline to them. But before they hung up, they gave me a shock with this instruction, "The Saturday evening service starts at 6:00, so you need to be here at 3:00."

"What for?" I asked.

"Well, we have a team meeting before the service, and we need you to be a part of it."

So I arrived at the suggested time. They took me up in the "crow's nest" office. As a team, the staff and I went through my sermon including illustrations. They were already familiar with the material I faxed them. Then the team offered creative suggestions; one lady said, "I think you need to change this word here. It doesn't seem to say exactly what you want."

Though I was not accustomed to such help and accountability, I replied, "That's a fine improvement."

communicated better because I had an entire team helping me get the message across.

Then just before we went into service, we had a meeting with everyone who had anything to do in the service. We discussed each individual's responsibility. Then we prayed together and went out to do the service.

Following the service, someone said, "There's more. We're going to have a meeting to critique the service." So on Saturday night we talked over each component of the service to see how we could improve it for the next day.

Coming away from that experience, I knew I had experienced much more creativity for that message than most of my sermons. I communicated better because I had an entire team helping me get the message across. The team supported me spiritually. That was a new experience for me, but I liked it very much.

This approach illustrates the power of what a team can do working together on every phase of ministry. With more thought and creativity, team support could be used to enrich most phases of ministry. Like a rising tide in a harbor, every ministry improves when a spirit of togetherness and improvement flows throughout the leadership of your church.

HABIT 4—BE A PEOPLE PERSON

People are the church's main business. Without people there can be no church. Cherish people. Laugh and cry with people. Listen to their fears, failings, and feelings. Value their affirmations and rejoice in their potential. Keep remembering the Savior established His Church for them.

Remember that nearly every believer wants to do something important for God but either does not know how or has not been challenged. They are not nearly as lethargic as many pastors think. Many church members want to follow a pastor but too often do not know where the pastor is going. A pastor will be more effective if he or she takes time to consider how people think, to understand how people respond, and to discover why people attend church.

Advice from President Eisenhower

President Dwight D. Eisenhower once said, "Leadership is the ability to get a person to do what you want him to do, when you want it done, in a way you want it done, because he wants to do it." We pastors need to hear something else that Eisenhower said: "You don't lead people by hitting them over the head; any fool can do that, but that is usually called *assault,* not *leadership.*"

But should assault—verbal or emotional—be tolerated in the fellowship our Lord expects to be cherished in the church? Though we have read and preached about agape love, in too many places pastors act as if they are duty bound to order people around. Some scold. Others berate. In still other settings, pastors shame people into doing what they want done. A wonderfully faithful layman recently observed, "Our new pastor hates people."

Love Them into Effective Service

There's a story from a quiet little girl that helps me be a loving leader of people. Twelve-year-old Sally took her younger brother, who was mentally handicapped, Christmas shopping. As they went into a department store, they passed a clerk who was overtired from long hours during the Christmas rush. The boy bumped a rack, knocking shoes in every direction.

Then the clerk grabbed the boy by the arm and demanded, "Pick them up."

"No," the boy screamed with defiance.

"Pick them up," the clerk shouted.

"No," the boy shouted back.

The big sister began picking up shoes. The boy started to help. Before long, the boy, his sister, and the overtired clerk were working together to get the shoes back in order.

When they finished, the girl taught the clerk a profound

lesson with these words, "Mister, you have to love my brother into doing it."

The story provides a bigger-than-life parable for leaders in today's church. People are the main business of the church, and they have to be loved into doing it.

That's an important formula for every pastor from the sister in the story—people cannot be made to do anything. One pastor remarked, "Been there. Tried that. It doesn't work." I wish every pastor would repeat these words over and over in the outworking of their ministry: "I can't make people do anything."

HABIT 5—WINNING ATTITUDE

After studying many leaders, it is obvious to me that most have a special attitude inside them. Call it possibility thinking, passion, positive thinking, energized focus, or vital faith. Whatever the label, these leaders believe God wants to help them accomplish the impossible. Church history provides examples by the hundreds. Every church that desires explosive growth must have someone near the top of their team who believes and communicates an attitude that expects and experiences miracles.

Keep Away from Negative Thinkers

Never, never surrender your vision to negative thinkers. Every church has a member or two who always see the gloomy side of an issue or see an attack dog behind every bush. These

You must realize that a glass ceiling can be put on an entire congregation by a few negative thinkers.

dear brothers and sisters have to be loved, accepted, and served as persons for whom Christ died. You must realize that a glass ceiling can be put on an entire congregation by a few negative thinkers. Be pastoral to them, but do not allow them to pollute your spirit or contaminate your faith. Since negative thinkers usually do not or cannot change much, it is usually not advisable to spend much time trying to fix them.

Remember what the children of Israel did the day after they crossed the Red Sea? They opened a branch office of the negative thinkers' society by complaining, "Moses, why did you bring us out here? We want to go back and be slaves." They could not see what God was doing. They had trouble remembering what God had done for them in the past and had no awareness of what He wanted to do for them then.

Initiate ways to keep individuals with destructive attitudes from setting the direction for your congregation. They cannot be allowed to shape the agenda for your ministry. They must not be permitted to erect emotional land mines under what God wants you to do in your assignment.

As leader, you can usually counteract negative attitudes by communicating vision and feeding faith to the whole church. That requires that you look beyond crises, circumstances, hindrances, or pain. That means you see success when it is only a tiny glimmer of light at the end of a dark tunnel. That means you purposefully keep company with positive, believing people. That means you see potential more than problems.

You must move your congregation from difficulty to hope, frustration to faith, and from problems to solutions. You must move the people from accepting circumstances as they are to expecting miracles from God.

HABIT 6—BALANCED LIFE

Most of my life, I have worked hard to be a balanced leader. To this day, this goal sometimes seems like a moving target. Balance is rooted in a leader's attitude about being a well-rounded Christian. Two Bible verses especially help me with this issue.

Those painful events changed me forever, so my order of priorities are God, family, and church.

One morning, I woke up at 6:33 and the Lord brought Matt. 6:33 to my mind. Remember what it says? "Seek ye first the kingdom of God, and his righteousness; and all these things shall be added unto you" (KJV). That is the foundation of genuine balance for ministers—"seek first."

For me, efforts at balance start with crystal-clear priorities concerning my family. God, church, and family were my dad's order of priorities. But I believe if he lived today, he would reorder those priorities. I went through a tragic loss in 1970 when I thought I was doing my best for God. Those painful events changed me forever, so my order of priorities are God, family, and church. The essentials to which I am committed are the same as Dad's, but order of family and church have changed places.

How does that work out in the details? I take the verse that says, "Let love be your greatest aim" (1 Cor. 14:1, TLB) as my foundation for these priorities. I have a standard rule—no matter what I'm doing—if my wife or children call, they get through immediately—no putting them on hold, no making them call back, and no waiting. Now, I may be in a serious conference like marriage counseling where I need to say to my son, "Scott, how are you doing today? I'm glad you called. Where are you? I have somebody in my office I really need to share with a little longer. Can I call you right back?" Then when I am finished, I call him immediately.

What am I doing? I am providing an expression of balance and priority that speaks volumes to my family and to my congregation. I am saying to my family, "You are the most important people in my life." That is what they are. That is what they need to know. And that is what I need to remember to tell them. I love saying to one of my children when we are in the car together, "You know, I love to pastor this church, but you are more important than the church to me." They like to hear that, and I like to hear myself say it.

An unexpected though significant ministry serendipity comes from this practice. Those who observe me putting my family first are more likely to put their family first. They follow my lead, and less family counseling is needed because fewer family crises occur in our congregation.

As part of our commitment to balance, my wife and I set regular times on our calendar where we get away from everything together. The larger our church became, the bigger the problem got. So we set times, maybe a day, maybe two days, sometimes three days, when we get away from everybody and just have fun together. Since I am in ministry for the long run, I want to enjoy meaningful family relationships at every stage in my journey.

Healthy Church Growth

I believe Rick Warren is right to suggest our need is to develop healthy churches. Unhealthy churches may grow for a while, but they soon wither or become handicapped. But really healthy churches grow. After a while, unhealthy churches self-destruct and their leaders wreck.

Being a leader of a healthy church means keeping your life balanced by building loving relationships with those closest to you. Then, a healthy ministry that is whole and authentic can last through all the good times and the hard times too. And healthy leaders will lead healthy churches that will eventually grow because they are well and whole.

HABIT 7—NEVER GIVE UP

The last one is special for me—never quit. When the going gets tough, with Christ's help, the tough get going. The "achiever's creed" is this: "Whatever the mind can conceive, and I will dare to believe, with God's help I can achieve."

I've been shipwrecked three times, and immersed in the open sea for a night and a day."

From Bible times to today, God's people have always faced obstacles that could cause them to give up. The apostle Paul, for example, said that he had been "beaten up more times than I can count, and at death's door time after time. I've been flogged five times with the Jews' thirty-nine lashes, beaten by Roman rods three times, pummeled with rocks once. I've been shipwrecked three times, and immersed in the open sea for a night and a day. In hard traveling year in and year out, I've had to ford rivers, fend off robbers, struggle with friends, struggle with foes. I've been at risk in the city, at risk in the country, endangered by desert sun and sea storm, and betrayed by those I thought were my brothers. I've known drudgery and hard labor, many a long and lonely night without sleep, many a missed meal, blasted by the cold, naked to the weather. And that's not the half of it, when you throw in the daily pressures and anxieties of all the churches" (2 Cor. 11:23-28, TM).

Yet Paul did not turn back. He fought the good fight. He was faithful to the heavenly vision. He learned that God's grace is enough. "It's all you need," God told him (2 Cor. 12:9, TM).

J. Hudson Taylor, pioneer missionary to China, wrote, "All God's giants have been weak men who did great things for God because they reckoned on His being with them." The apostle Paul—thanks to his poor health, his tendency to cause riots, and

had no way of knowing how God would heal my brokenness and turn it into a blessing.

perhaps his prison record—would have been rejected by many churches and mission boards today. But God used him in a remarkable way. Why? Instead of quitting, he learned how to be empowered by God. "When I am weak, then I am strong," he said (2 Cor. 12:10) and "I can do all things through Christ who strengthens me" (Phil. 4:13, NJKV).

It is through hardship that God prepares us for the more difficult, more responsible places of leadership. I recall lying on a beach in Oregon in 1970, crying out to God in gut-wrenching pain. My world had been devastated. Everything inside me wanted to quit. I had no way of knowing how God would heal my brokenness and turn it into a blessing.

But He did. Out of pain, He brought gain. Out of ashes, He brought beauty. The key verse for me is Gen. 50:20: "You intended to harm me, but God intended it for good to accomplish what is now being done, the saving of many lives." There is no growth without struggle.

I heard of a sixth-grade boy who collected several cocoons and stored them in his attic. Each day he would look for signs of breakthrough. One afternoon, he got to watch the miracle of life unfolding. He watched the newly formed butterfly struggle with intense difficulty to break out of its shell. First it opened up a little hole. Then with great effort, it enlarged the hole. At last the butterfly emerged, fluttered its wings, and flew off.

The boy thought he had a bright idea. He would save the others from such a struggle. When the next butterfly was trying to emerge from its cocoon, he cut a large hole so it could come through quickly into the new world. Unfortunately, without those hours of struggle, the butterfly never gained the strength it needed to fly as it was intended.

In a similar way, struggles give us strength to fly higher, to become what God created us to be. God has placed resources within us that we can discover only through struggles and hardship. Strength, both physical and spiritual, is the product of struggle. That is why it is so important never to give up.

◾5◾

BUILDING BRIDGES, RALLYING SUPPORT FOR THE VISION

How to Get Key Opinion Leaders on Board

by Maxie D. Dunnam

Charles Schultz, one of my favorite cartoonists and theologians, knows a lot about life and church. In a recent series, he has Lucy—that bossy, assertive, always-take-control character—playing her role as psychiatrist. She sits in her booth with a banner on the top that says "Psychiatric Help—5 cents," and then down below a sign says, "The Doctor Is In." Charlie Brown is her patient. Lucy says to Charlie, "Your life is like a house . . ."

In the next frame, she says reflectively, "You want your house to have a solid foundation, don't you?" Charlie Brown has a kind of blank look on his face.

Almost casually, but as though she has to stay in control, in the next frame Lucy says, "Of course you do."

Charlie Brown is still silent—saying nothing. Then in the fourth frame, psychiatrist Lucy says, "So don't build your house on the sand, Charlie Brown." About that time, a huge wind comes up and it blows the psychiatrist's booth down. All you see is Lucy falling back with her signs "Psychiatric Help—5 cents" and "The Doctor Is In" covering her. In the final frame, she emerges from the rubble saying, "Or use cheap nails . . ."

That's biblical, of course. And it is a word for us who are called to ministry and who are committed to providing the very best leadership God would want His Church to have.

In this chapter, I want to deal with crucial issues in leadership—in any organization, but especially in the church—building bridges and rallying support.

81

If you have not come face-to-face with failure because of not paying attention to this issue, your day is coming. This problem is one of the most common causes of division in the Body of Christ, and a pastor can fix it fairly easily.

WHAT I LEARNED FROM STARTING A "ROCK AND ROLL" SERVICE

Last year, I received a Christmas card from a couple in Memphis. They are both retired now. Mary was an executive with one of the General Motors divisions—charming, alive, assertive, an achiever in every way. John was an accountant—a successful one—but the kind of fellow who could come and go in a room and you would never know he was there, a straight-laced, rigid sort of fellow.

John and Mary are both extremely traditional—not only in their social and cultural lives, but in their religious life. They were members of Christ Church for 30 years. They always attended the 11 A.M. service, which was as liturgical as most Methodist churches would get—wonderful choir, procession, what some would call "high church" music. Mary had even served on the music committee and was an ardent supporter of that kind of service.

I invite you to look over my shoulder at the handwritten message on their Christmas card. "We still miss you." And then this word: "We go to the Saturday 5:30 service—rock-'n'-roll. We're giving each other black leather jackets for Christmas. Now we need a motorcycle."

That was not only a signal to me about the kind of church I left behind but also showed that I was somewhat successful in building the kind of congregation that had vitality and continued to grow "after Maxie."

We started that 5:30 Saturday night seekers' service about six months before I left Christ Church. We had two worship services when I went to Christ Church, an 8:30 service and an eleven o'clock service. There was little difference between the 8:30 and the eleven o'clock service except the 8:30 service did not have the full choir and the bells and whistles of that kind of service. But still it was rather straight and formal.

We brought in a consultant—George Hunter, who is on faculty here at Asbury. We asked him to talk about evangelism and out-reach—to help us in visioning our future. He said one thing that caught our attention. That was that anytime a congregation added a new worship service they could count on increasing their worship attendance by at least 10 percent. We wanted to serve more people, but our eleven o'clock service had reached its capacity. I knew we could not change the 8:30 service because it had a core of about 150 people there who were committed to that style of service.

Anytime a congregation added a new worship service they could count on increasing their worship attendance by at least 10 percent.

So we made the decision that we would start a 9:45 Sunday worship service. We worked with the worship committee and the Council on Ministries. We clearly communicated the concept that with the diverse population in Memphis, we needed to offer another service different from the two we had. The lay leadership of the church and decision makers were excited about the idea.

So we started a praise service at 9:45. We started in a chapel that would seat 350. The first Sunday we packed in 400 people. We kept the service there for only about six weeks and then moved it to the fellowship hall. We didn't want to move it to the sanctuary because we felt that setting did not lend itself to the kind of praise service we wanted. That service over a period of time grew to be almost as large as the eleven o'clock worship service. We were having between 900 and 1,000 people in that service when I left.

Next we started a Saturday night service. We began to feel that with the 9:45 and eleven o'clock services packed and with the 8:30 service reasonably attended we ought to do two things.

First, we should make the 8:30 service more children and family friendly. And that's the one service when we had a children's sermon. I think we sometimes forget that parents of little children have to get up early on Sunday morning because children don't sleep in on Sunday like adults do. Why not provide a service for them that would fit more easily into their schedule? So we turned that service, with the total support of the congregation, into a children-friendly service.

But we also thought we had to have another outreach service that was radically different from the 9:45 Sunday morning service. So we began to build consensus and enthusiasm about it. We decided that it would be a totally different service that would reflect the unique music sound of Memphis. As part of the start-up, I asked for 150 people from the three Sunday services who would be willing to attend that service for three months to be a welcoming body for outsiders. I asked for 150, and we got more than 200. Then we started that service. It uses instrumentalists called The Lord's Most Dangerous Band with some of the city's best musicians who have Memphis blues sound. People from all walks of life attend.

Well, my Christmas card from Mary and John shows the success of that service. These two straight, traditional, eleven o'clock worshiping members are now a dynamic part of that Saturday night service, which they call "rock-'n'-roll." So you understand the joy that is mine when they write with wonderful humor that they are going to get leather jackets for Christmas and buy a motorcycle.

The key to effectiveness in starting the radically different Saturday night service was the way we built bridges and rallied support.

WHAT I LEARNED FROM STARTING A HEALING SERVICE

Now let me tell you a failure story.

When I first went to Christ Church, two people on our staff, a husband and wife, were Dale and Sandra Brady. Dale was our minister of recreation and Sandra was our part-time youth minister. Sandra had cancer that was in and out of remission, but she was not able to function with much enthusiasm and energy. She was a wonderful young woman, beloved in that congregation.

Since I am deeply committed to prayer and believe in healing, I thought we should pray for Sandra's healing. I strongly believe the church should pray for healing. I do not think a healing ministry ought to be left to individuals, though I am sure some individuals have been anointed for that particular ministry. Though I have not been anointed to this ministry, I believe the church is called to it.

So about three months after I arrived at Christ Church,

without reflecting too much about it, I decided we ought to have a healing service for Sandra. She was at the heart of that congregation. Everybody knew her. Everybody loved her. I felt it was the thing to do. So we did it. One Sunday we announced it. It was held in Reeve's Chapel; 100 people came. Since Sandra was in the hospital, I invited the lay leader of the church to come and sit in proxy for her. Some of us gathered round him, laid hands on him, and prayed for Sandra in that symbolic way.

Well, I'm not exaggerating when I say chaos ensued. Meetings were held. Forces began to be garnered. People called on me. You would have thought Oral Roberts had come to town. Many people wanted to get rid of me because they thought I was too charismatic or too Pentecostal. It was a rough time.

But level heads prevailed. People began to know who I was and the opposition couldn't garner enough support to move me. So I stayed—but here's the tragic thing. As a result of that incident, I did not feel I could start a public ministry of healing for a long time. It wasn't until almost 10 years had passed before we finally started a 5:30 Sunday afternoon healing service. That service, a service of healing prayer and holy communion, is still going on.

What caused the difference in the two outcomes?

How to Build Bridges and Rally Support

The difference between the successful start-up of the Saturday night service and near disaster concerning Sandra's healing service was my failure to give attention to building bridges and rallying support. The techniques are not nearly as important as the process and a pastor's commitment to seeing that it is done.

Use Accountability to Shape Use of Pastoral Power

Every pastor has a significant amount of power, which is rooted in God's call to ministry, ordination, lay respect for clergy, installment as the head of a specific congregation, and from one's personal piety. But unless authentic accountability is in place, pastoral power never helps us build a bridge or rally support. As a starting point in building support, a pastor must use power in ways that are pleasing to Christ and acceptable to fair-minded people.

Above almost everything else, a pastor must make an undisputed, voluntary commitment to be responsibly accountable. Accountability always starts by recognizing leaders need a circle of people in their lives with whom they feel safe to share openly and honestly. The church does not work well when led by dictators or pseudomessiahs. That is why every pastor needs a caring, responsible group of people with whom everything can be laid on the table. Such a group should be encouraged to be candidly forthright with a leader. Ministers need someone to question them about relationships, motives, time use, and money.

> *he church does not work well when led by dictators or pseudomessiahs.*

Too often, almost weekly, ministers hear about colleagues who are glaring examples of misused power, who refuse to be accountable, and who have wrecked their ministry. As a result, many go wrong and become morally or vocationally crippled for life. Then all ministers get discredited. As a result, laypersons are often devastated spiritually even as congregations are ruined.

Check Your Motives

When we exercise power in leadership, we need to be alert to the motives that are governing what we do and the ends or purposes for which we use our power. Lord Acton's assertion "Power tends to corrupt; absolute power corrupts absolutely" is something we must always keep in mind.

We need to acknowledge that Acton is often misquoted. He didn't say power corrupts; he said that power *tends* to corrupt—it is absolute power that corrupts absolutely, and that is the reason we need to exercise power in the context of an effective system of accountability. Asking yourself "Why did I use authority the way I did?" is the right question. And the right answer is "To please God and serve people for God's glory."

When Christian leaders think of power and authority, accountability and trust in the context of leadership, it is well that we remember Jesus' word recorded in Mark 10:42-44: "You know that those who are regarded as rulers of the Gentiles lord it over them, and their high officials exercise authority over them.

Not so with you. Instead, whoever wants to become great among you must be your servant, and whoever wants to be first must be slave of all."

Dangerous or Useful Power

In her book *The Religion of Power,* Cheryl Forbes discusses the concept of power. In her way of thinking, power is defined as follows: "Insistence on what we want for no other reason than that we want it; it means making other people follow us despite their own wishes. Power is assumed, insensitive, dehumanizing, and ultimately destructive."

As you can see from that definition, Forbes sees power as something to be "delivered from" rather than something to be sought. "Christians must say no to power," Forbes insists, "individually and corporately. A decision for power is antithetical to a desire for God."

I believe power is not something to be shunned. Rather it is to be used in the context of total Christian commitment and in the context of leadership committed to Kingdom enterprises.

Christian Authority and Spiritual Leader

Interestingly, Forbes contrasts power and authority. She sees authority in a very positive way, saying that it usually involves a conferred right within strictly controlled bounds. She says it is temporary recognition or a temporary state of *"in charge-ness."* So, there are two huge issues related to leadership and how we build bridges and rally support.

One issue is authority in connection with leadership. When a pastor is installed as head of a congregation, he or she is automatically given some degree of ecclesiastical authority. In many congregations and denominations, the ordination charge says "take thou authority." This kind of authority is to preach the Word of God, administer sacraments, and lead a congregation— all significant issues for the church.

Note, however, that no IBM or General Motors executive needs, possesses, or uses any of those authorities. That's the point of difference. The pastor does significant things that marketplace leaders never do. The source of our authority is different from theirs. We are ministers of Christ, not corporate moguls.

In his book *Who Speaks for God*, Chuck Colson says that "power and authority must not be confused. Power is the ability to affect one's ends or purposes in the world. Authority is having not only the power (might) but the right to affect one's purpose. Power is often maintained by naked force; and authority springs from a moral foundation. Mother Teresa is the best living example. She spends her life helping the powerless die with dignity; yet few people command more authority world-wide."

Colson cautions us that worldly power, whether measured by buildings, budgets, baptisms, or access to the White House, is more often the enemy than the ally of godliness.

> *All the authority we have must be exercised in the consciousness that we are emissaries of Jesus.*

For us Christian leaders, the issue is neither an undue concern for power for its own sake nor authority for its own sake because we cease being Christian when that becomes the case. Rather the issue is, how can I exercise God-given power and authority to help the organization He has entrusted to me achieve His purposes and goals? All the authority we have, if we're exercising it as Christian leaders, must be exercised in the consciousness that we are emissaries of Jesus—we represent Him.

Ponder the meaning of being an emissary of Jesus. All power you receive from your Lord, the church, and any other source must be exercised with Judgment-Day awareness that you are an emissary of Jesus. Live by the principle. The Christian leader is as much a representative for Jesus in board meetings as in a pulpit.

MINISTRY MUST BE BUILT ON TRUST

Trust is the glue that holds a church together. Few things are more essential for rallying support and building bridges. Face this important fact—trust is fully as important as authority or power for a Christian leader. I was saddened when the *Indianapolis Star* printed an article on the front page in a Sunday edition titled "Faith Betrayed." The headline, which was likely written by a secular journalist, captures our attention, doesn't it? This article was a part of a series about betrayal of trust in the Lafayette diocese of the Roman Catholic Church in Indiana. The problems were horrendous and the newspaper, of course, wanted to make the story as dramatic as possible. Essentially the issue was trust had been destroyed. Without trust, ministry grinds to a halt.

Trust Can Be Easily Sabotaged

Trust is amazingly fragile. The history of many congregations demonstrates how misdirected ambition, immorality, dishonesty, stubbornness, selfishness, and putting personal interests first undermine trust. One stupid act or one impure attitude can wipe out years of effective trust building.

At the same time, several less obvious attitudes and practices also undermine trust.

• **Either/or thinking.** Trust is diminished and vision blurred when either/or thinking is used in planning or decision making. This happens when a leader presents an issue as though only one viable option for a decision exists. Decisions get short-circuited in such an environment. Then committees and boards are hindered from exploring alternatives and kept from learning to move through difficult situations.

Symbolically, it is always a bad move to use either/or thinking. When laypersons see it practiced by clergy leaders, followers start using the same faulty reasoning. Then before you realize it, either/or kind of strategy pushes people to make divisive choices between young versus old, big givers versus small givers, old-timers versus newcomers, and new converts versus veteran church members. An either/or mind-set undercuts trust in the work of the church because it polarizes people, issues, and results. Our creative God can be counted on to provide many more options, solutions, and choices than either/or thinking allows.

• **Suspect data and facts.** Sometimes trust can be subverted when hard data or facts are allowed to overrun feelings and intuition. This can happen easily when minister or lay leader goes to a board with a long list of convincing facts and figures. Because they have hard data to support their recommendations, they expect decision makers to follow their suggestions. The problem— they ignore feelings and disregard intuitions, which play such a large part in shaping so many decisions in any church.

The truth of the matter is that sometimes our intuitions and feelings are far more important in decision making than data. I can't think of too many situations in my own ministry when we have moved forward in a dynamic and creative way when we had all the data and facts to support what we were doing. More often than not, the leading of the Spirit, the feelings that we had about conditions that existed, and intuitions about direction of ministry guided our actions.

Do not put too much weight on facts alone, but count on the motivating power of a dream or the inspiring power of a vision. But that inspiration must always be shared to build bridges and rally support.

Consistency Nourishes Trust

A leader's steadiness is among the most effective ways trust is developed. I learned lessons about steadiness early in my ministry during the civil rights struggles in the early '60s in Mississippi. I remember as if it happened yesterday. Some of us pastors had issued a public statement about race relationships. All the forces of the devil went to work in the community and church.

After I had been questioned past midnight, a lay leader raised the tough question that was on everyone's mind: "Well, preacher, what can we expect of you in the future?"

As if inspired by God, I quietly answered, "You can expect me to be consistent."

I really believe steadfastness is among the biggest factors that determine whether people trust a pastor. They don't feel comfortable trusting a leader who waffles. But they are attracted by steadfastness and integrity.

Fairness Nourishes Trust

Fairness is another important component in building trust. The people who make up the congregation must be able to trust you to be fair in public as well as in the back room at the kitchen cabinet. A reputation for fairness is built by being fair, time after time and in all relationships.

Fairness is a quality of character that is usually returned to a leader in the same measure as it is given. Learn to give the benefit of the doubt to others. Allow people in your decision groups, on your staff, and in the congregation to count on you to keep stretching your heart and mind to be fair on every issue.

KEEP THEOLOGY OF THE CHURCH CLEAR AND ALIVE

What you believe about the church profoundly affects everything you do in ministry. A theology of the church forms a dynamic cornerstone for all the rest to be built on. Biblical images of the church provide an understanding that shapes your mission and ministry.

The New Testament offers incredibly inspiring images of the church that are so exhilarating they keep us going when things get boring, when people misunderstand us, or when a congregation's mission gets out of focus. These biblical concepts need to be the foundation on which a congregation's understanding of its life and work is built.

Those Magnificent People of God

The first biblical image on which we developed ministry at Christ Church was the church as the people of God. Scripture teaches in 1 Pet. 2, "You are a chosen race, a royal priesthood, a holy nation, God's own people, that you may declare the wonderful deeds of him who called you out of darkness into his marvelous light. Once you were no people but now you're God's people; once you had not received mercy but now you have received mercy" (vv. 9-10, RSV). What a solid cornerstone for everything a church is called to be and do.

A Magnetic Fellowship

When you think of the church as the people of God, you almost automatically think about fellowship that truly matters. This is a holy togetherness that gives a sense of belonging and produces robust relationships that are stronger than ties to natural kin.

I am coming to believe about fellowship and belonging that a congregation in our day is to be an evangelist to the world, showing them what they are missing. What I mean is that what goes on in a congregation draws people to Christ. Relationships are so healthy and attractive that those outside the Kingdom want to become a disciple of Christ like the folks at church. This attraction in a church is Christlikeness lived out among

God's people so outsiders become curious, even hungry for
Him.

It is something like curiosity produced by a five-alarm fire
but multiplied a million times. I love the story about an occasion
when the eccentric actress Tallulah Bankhead went to worship at
St. Mary the Divine Episcopal Church in New York City. Some
say St. Mary's is so liturgical that Roman Catholics go there to
visit to see how it was before the reforms of Vatican II. In the
worship service that morning, there was a grand processional
with triumphant music. Following the choir came the bishop in
gem-studded robes, waving a censer that emitted incense smoke.
As the story goes, Tallulah Bankhead was seated on the end of a
pew. When the old bishop came near her, she tugged at his robe.
After she got his attention, she said in her gravelly voice,
"Dahling, your gown is divine but your purse is on fire." Though
we want an attractive, redemptive fire in the church, it is not that
kind we seek.

To use Elton Trueblood's term, an incendiary fellowship is
needed that is so empowered by the Holy Spirit that persons are
attracted to it. Then when people come within the influence of
the church, there will be some redemptive drawing that takes
place in their mind and heart.

The Body of Christ—a Continuing Presence

Another biblical metaphor that moved ministry forward at
Christ Church was the church as the Body of Christ. While the
people of God image calls a congregation to redemptive fellowship, healthy relationships, caring friendships, magnetic hospitality, and delightful belonging, the Body of Christ image from
Scripture suggests serving and servanthood.

*Serving is the most
impressive image of Christ
in the New Testament.*

Serving is the most impressive image of Christ in the New
Testament. Think of the meaning and implications. In the Bible,
the Savior graciously becomes servant, the Son of God volunteers to be a love slave, and the Lord willingly washes feet. He

announces, "I have come among you to serve." And our Lord redefined greatness forever with that startling announcement.

At Christ Church—sometimes successfully and sometimes not so successfully—we deliberately sought to minister to the poor. Our efforts included ministry at the jail and housing ministry. That congregation now builds two houses for the poor each year. That's the sort of thing that I mean—a deliberate effort to serve the poor in the name of Jesus without any thought or hope of return.

Biblical Images Must Shape Decisions

When these New Testament images are kept before a congregation, the scriptural concepts, expectations, and promises become the reference point for a congregation's work and offer a sound biblical framework for decision making. Such authentic grappling with the issues helps a congregation see what God is calling a church to be and do. In the process, biblical ideals clarify and energize our work for God. Then when biblically based decisions are made, it takes heat off the minister. Now he or she is no longer the only one who says, "This is what we ought to do. There is where we ought to go."

Let's take some more instruction and inspiration from *Peanuts*.

Linus, holding his blanket, is defeated and downcast. He's walking along followed by Charlie Brown who tries to snap him out of despair.

Charlie questions Linus, "What if everybody was like you? What if we all ran away from our problems, huh? What then?"

Charlie throws his hands up in a dramatic gesture as he asks, "What if everyone in the whole world decided to run away from his problems?"

Linus responds with insightful wisdom, "Well, at least we'd all be running in the same direction."

What is needed in almost every congregation is for pastor and people to be running in the same direction and that their direction be the direction God wants. That only happens if we keep the self-understanding of a congregation clearly true to Scripture.

MAINTAIN AND SHARPEN ORGANIZATIONAL PERSPECTIVE

It's very easy for leaders to become so focused on an issue at hand that they do not consider the congregation as a whole. We must constantly ask ourselves, "How does what I'm seeking to do affect the entire organization?"

A big issue is what I call an episodic approach to ministry planning. It is very easy for a church to cast its entire program into just that—programs—a series of episodic events that may or may not have any connection. For instance, a congregation can have a spring revival, a missions conference in the fall, a study emphasis during Lent, some sort of tremendous emphasis on Christmas music and Christmas programming during the Advent/Christmas season—just a series of episodes—but fail to design a holistic model for making disciples.

Developing Authentic Disciples

I remember at Christ Church when I became aware of the fact that we were approaching our program planning in that fashion and the limitation of it. We engaged our staff and the lay leadership of our church to address this issue. We came up with what we called a "design for discipleship." We wanted to try to move people along the road of discipleship. For instance, if they were at what they would think of as point C, maybe we could get them to point H—just to move them along in some deliberate way in their discipleship growth.

The driving notion of our design was this: "That Christians might be reasonably informed, reasonably inspired, and reasonably equipped." That design had four tracks: (1) spiritual discipline and growth, (2) Bible and theology, (3) applied discipleship, and (4) life concerns. For a period of time, until we developed an even more holistic and complete mission statement, everything we did was looked at through those lenses.

Get Some Distance

I have discovered in my own ministry that I cannot keep that organizational perspective, nor can I keep a theology of the church clear and alive, unless I pay close attention to my own personal mental, spiritual, and philosophical moods and perspectives.

In my last 12 years as a pastor, I had two practices that enabled me to maintain the organizational perspective and also to keep the theology of the church clear and alive.

One of those was regular retreats—24 hours, 36 hours, 48 hours. About every three or four months I would go away, just to be in retreat. Most of the time I would not take anything but my Bible and a tablet of paper. It was a time to pray, to think, to reflect, to look at the church, to let my soul and mind settle so I could be clearheaded and pure-hearted.

Balance Leadership and Management

Another essential dynamic of bridge building and support rallying is to keep a balance between leadership and management. Now oftentimes leaders will picture these in contrast—the difference between being a leader and a manager, and there is a difference. But I want to make the case for the idea that every leader must be a manager. Now every manager may not be a leader, but every leader should be a manager.

My reason is that I do not know any leader who does not have to do some managing. We do not get along very well or very long in our pastoral ministry without being able to manage people, being able to manage time, being able to administer programs.

We need to pay attention to management but not allow management to consume us or to take the place of leadership.

LISTENING AND HEARING PEOPLE

Still another dynamic of bridge building and support rallying is listening and hearing the people. Richard Mouw, the president of Fuller Theological Seminary, has written a marvelous little book titled *Consulting the Faithful*. The subtitle of that book is "What Christian Intellectuals Can Learn from Popular Religion." It is well worth your reading. He has one chapter that he calls the "sense of the faithful" in which he talks about the failure of the church—the whole church—to take into account the intuition and judgments of commonplace Christians.

I think it is one of the biggest sins of the church today that we simply do not trust laypersons when we are making decisions about the nature and mission of the church. I think it is very important for ministers, and pastors, to cultivate a sensitivity to laypeople, to be able to share with laypeople in such a way that they can get the sense of the faithful.

I'm not talking about everything being a matter of majority vote, and I'm not talking about catering to laypeople and to the prejudices and whims of laypeople. I'm talking about matters of faith and morality that have to do with mission and ministry.

BEARING ANOTHER'S BURDEN

The fifth essential dynamic of bridge building and support rallying is the ministry of bearing one another's burdens. I believe that we need to build congregations that are characterized by the mutual bearing of one another's burdens, with the clergy noticeably participating.

It is easy now for a senior pastor in a staff position to become further and further removed from pastoral involvement with people.

I remember when I was at Christ Church I had to make a decision about pastoral care. In a congregation that size, you can imagine that the senior minister cannot do pastoral counseling, pastoral visitation, and hospital visitation. I made a decision, though, to keep deliberate pastoral contact with the congregation. And I outlined a very specific way of doing it.

One, I set aside two afternoons a week when I would do pastoral care and counseling and would basically do that by appointment.

Two, I would call on the leadership of the church when they were hospitalized. Now that was a tricky kind of thing because it could very easily be seen as showing favoritism. But when I called on the leadership of the church who were in the hospital, I always called on all members of our congregation who were in the hospital at the same time.

Three, I took a number of the weddings and involved myself with premarital counseling.

Four, I took my turn preaching in the jail services that our church was responsible for, a ministry that my wife, Jerry, primarily led.

Five, I always attended the men's prayer breakfast on Friday morning.

Six, in my preaching, I was always confessional enough to

let the congregation know what was going on in my own life. In all my preaching and teaching and relationships, I tried to participate in the bearing of one another's burdens.

The larger the church gets, the more deliberate the senior minister must become in communicating this dimension of mutual burden bearing. If we share in the lives of people when they are hurting, and if we allow people to know that we hurt and allow some of them to share in our hurting, then we establish the foundation for a church that is a mutual burden-bearing community of faith.

The last three years I served at Christ Church, our congregation had become known as a place of hospitality for recovering folks. That could never have happened, and people would not have been willing to set aside huge space in our building and give a lot of energy to allowing that sort of dynamic to take place, had we not come to consciously understand that a part of the call to the church is that word of Paul in Galatians, "Bear one another's burdens, and so fulfill the law of Christ" (6:2, NKJV).

LEARN FROM MOTORCYCLES AND LAWNMOWERS

Let me summarize with a parable about Wes Seliger, an unconventional Episcopal clergyman who loves motorcycles. He tells about being in a motorcycle shop one day, drooling over a huge Honda 750 and wishing that he could buy it. A salesman came over and began to talk about his product. He talked about speed, acceleration, excitement, the attention-getting growl of the pipes, racing, risk. He talked about how the good-looking girls would be attracted to anyone riding on such a cycle.

Then he discovered that Wes was a minister. It always happens, doesn't it? Immediately the salesman changed his language and even the tone of his voice. He spoke quietly and talked about good mileage and visibility. It was indeed a "practical" vehicle.

Wes observed: "Lawnmower salespersons are not surprised to find clergypersons looking at their merchandise; motorcycle salespersons are. Why? Does this tell us something about clergypersons and about the church? Lawnmowers are slow, safe, sane, practical, and middle-class. Motorcycles are fast, dangerous, wild, thrilling." Then Wes asks a question: "Is being a Christian more like mowing a lawn or like riding a motorcycle?

Is the Christian life safe and sound or dangerous and exciting?" He concludes, "The common image of the church is pure lawn-mower—slow, deliberate, plodding. Our task is to take the church out on the open road, give it the gas, and see what the old baby will do!"

The person who is going to do that is the pastor. When the minister knows that his or hers is a divine commission, when the minister cultivates his or her share in the mystery, when the minister preaches with passion and conviction, as the old saints of the church used to say, "as one dying person to another dying person"—or as D. T. Niles said, "as one starving beggar telling another beggar where to get bread"—we will discover again "what the old baby will do," and the church will come alive to be God's redemptive instrument in the world.

Put on your helmet, start your engine, rev up the throttle. Let's see what the church can do!

= 6 =

DISCOVERING AND EVALUATING VISIONARY LEADERS

People Development Is Exciting Business

by John Maxwell

In *The Leadership Lessons of Jesus,* Bob Briner and Rex Pritchard provide an insightful foundation for evaluating leaders: "Effective leaders constantly evaluate their followers. They must look for substance and avoid being fooled by the person who spends more time trying to look good than doing good." And they are right—the church needs substance.

Developing an effective church staff provides incredible possibilities for expanding ministry.

Developing an effective church staff provides incredible possibilities for expanding ministry. Simultaneously, however, it opens the door to potential hazards and can cause high stress levels for a pastor. But significant growth and a quality ministry, except in smallest churches, cannot be accomplished without staff. These realities mean every pastor must learn to effectively evaluate present and prospective leaders, including paid personnel and volunteer workers. The competence, character, commitment, and vision of your staff shape almost everything else about your church.

Dale Galloway states the commitment and process so well when he says, "Build leaders and leaders will build ministries." Jesus gave us this pattern when He concentrated on a select small group to achieve amazing results. But the results started

99

with choosing the right persons and evaluating them constantly and accurately.

This need for evaluation creates a dilemma for pastors, however, because recruiting and evaluating are not usually taught in college or seminary. It is tough, hard, complicated work. And it is not a natural gift for most pastors. But I have good news for you—evaluation strategies are reasonably easy to cultivate in a pastor's network of skills when the key ingredients are recognized and routinely used. Always remember you see clearly only what you are prepared to evaluate.

A GOOD LAUGH ABOUT STAFF ISSUES

To get this recruitment and evaluation process in focus, I enjoy laughing about what each church staff person should be expected to accomplish. I do not recall where this list originated, but perhaps the author would like to forget it too.

A senior pastor should be able to leap over tall buildings in a single bound. He should be more powerful than a locomotive and faster than a speeding bullet. He must walk on water and give policies to God.

An associate pastor should be able to leap over short buildings in a single bound. He should be as powerful as a switch engine and just as fast as a speeding bullet. He walks on water if the sea is calm and talks with God.

A minister of education should be able to leap over short buildings with a running start. He is nearly as powerful as a switch engine and faster than a speeding B.B. He walks on water if he knows where the stumps are and talks with God if a special request is approved by the senior pastor.

A minister of music should be able to clear a quonset hut, loses a race with a locomotive, can fire a speeding bullet, swims well, and is occasionally addressed by God.

A minister of single adults runs into small buildings, recognizes locomotives two out of three times, owns a squirt gun, knows how to use the water fountain, and mumbles to himself.

A church secretary lifts buildings to walk under them, kicks locomotives off the track, catches speeding bullets in her teeth, freezes water with a single glance, and when God speaks, she says, "May I ask who is calling?"

BEGIN WITH THE BASICS

Your effectiveness as a pastor and your personal growth as a leader run on two tracks of continual improvement. The first track is development of yourself as an effective leader across a lifetime. Its main traits are holy character, personal credibility, and a desire for personal competence. Use every means to develop yourself—books, seminars, case studies, evaluations, videos, mentors, and conversations with proven leaders. Though capable subordinates may be civil to a weak leader, they never seriously follow someone whose character they do not respect and whose skills they consider to be bumbling, rusty, or incompetent.

 *se every means to develop yourself.*

Track two requires you to develop others into leaders. Over a period of time as you put your energy and imagination on the line to develop staff members, you gain believability, they realize you are serious about quality, and they appreciate your commitments to them and to the gospel.

Never minimize or neglect the two-track growth concept. Both tracks can be developed simultaneously and continually. It is not one track but two. But how? How do we help others develop as we develop ourselves?

HOW TO EQUIP OTHERS

To get an effective handle on staff development, start by formulating an acrostic built on the word *equip*.

E = Evaluate

The key question: How well can they do?

The first requirement of accurate evaluation is to pick good people. Pastors, in seeking to build a great church, sometimes make the mistake of appointing people to lead in the same way the country bumpkin entered his crippled old mule in the Kentucky Derby. His friends laughed. His family ridiculed him. His critics razzed him and told him over and over that his mule had no chance to win the race. Finally, in response to the pressures to defend his actions, he said, "I know my mule can't win, but I thought the association might do him some good." His mistaken idea offers an important lesson for us in staff development: it is generally true that low potential results in low performance. That is why your evaluation of potential staff during the recruitment stage is absolutely crucial.

In all recruiting efforts, keep reminding yourself that no matter how much you help a person develop who is a 4 on the potential scale of 1 to 10, all you will ever have is a 4. You may succeed in taking such a person to the top of his or her potential, but he or she is still only a highly developed four. So accurate evaluation of staff members is necessary both while you are recruiting them and after they are added to the team.

Q = Qualify

The key question: How well do they do?

You must develop formal and informal ways to measure performance. Informal conversations give some clues. Regular reviews will provide factual data. Try listening to those whom this person's ministry touches. Note what other staffers say, even in jest, about this individual. Listen for what others do not say about this person. During this stage, do not rush to where you defend the staff person to his peers, or the others will simply shut down the information flow you need for evaluation.

Develop measurable ways to assure yourself that every staff member is developing his or her potential and planning ways to implement new and effective ministries. Some pastors ask staff members to give them monthly, quarterly, and annual written reports. Others ask each staff member to prepare an annual growth contract that shows in detail how the staff person plans to develop himself or herself. Such reports may seem like a bother, but when things go badly, they can be a marvelous lifesaver.

U = Unite

The key question: How well can we do together?

This means you faithfully and creatively put what you can do beside what they can do. This is the Kingdom law of complementary gifts—yours, theirs, and other members of the staff. Develop friendships with your staff members. Show them in every way possible that you want them to grow as individuals as well as professional leaders in the church. All this creates a dynamic synergism; then a near miraculous multiplication of results takes place. It is much more than 1 plus 1 equals 2—it is more like 1 plus 1 equals 10.

Develop friendships with your staff members.

I = Invest

The key question: Am I getting a return?

To help a staff member become all he or she can be requires a pastor to invest time, energy, resources, and confidence. This is easy to overlook because one of the main reasons for adding a staff member is that the senior pastor and others already have too much to do. Thus, when a staff member comes on board, others often quickly move back to their primary work and leave the new person to pick up the pieces. Such a situation is an understandable and common mistake that needs to be corrected.

Here's why investment is so important. Often a new staff member is confused, even lonely. Sometimes she does not understand what is expected or what to expect. And laypeople are sometimes slow in accepting her. Lots of long-term problems start by bringing a new staff member into a congregation and expecting her to find her own way. Even though she may survive, her ministry will not be resourceful or satisfying.

The senior pastor should wisely view such a commitment as an investment in the staff member's future achievement.

P = Provide

The key question: How can I help them do better?

"P" means provide—resources, personnel, equipment, and continuing training for staff members. As an example, it is a common mistake to install a minister of music without providing funds for new music or worship seminars.

Other churches have mistakenly engaged ministers of education without providing funds for literature, purchasing necessary audiovisual equipment, providing adequate classroom space, or furnishing sufficient office support.

Like carpenters, plumbers, and pastors, staff members

cannot do their work without tools or a crew. And if they try, their progress will be disappointingly slow and their morale moody.

If you implement the five verbs represented by the EQUIP acrostic, the results will be a church where staffers know their assignment and feel empowered to accomplish it. Then you will develop sturdy relationships with staff members so they will never want to work with anyone else. Meanwhile, you will experience joy in developing capable and dedicated people. At the same time, you will eliminate pounding migraine headaches caused by frequent staff turnovers. When a pastor commits to EQUIP when recruiting and developing leaders, the spirit of the church will be upbeat, positive, and faith building.

FIVE STEPS TO DEVELOPING KEY LEADERS

1. Check Attitudes—Yours and Theirs

Let us be sure we are on the same page about attitudes. I wrote this description years ago; it's what I mean when I use the word *attitude*:

It is the "advance man" of our true selves.

Its roots are inward but its fruit is outward.

It is our best friend or our worst enemy.

It is more honest and more consistent than our words.

It is an outward look based on past experiences.

It is a thing that draws people to us or repels them.

It is never content until it is expressed.

It is the librarian of our past.

It is the speaker of our present.

It is the prophet of our future.

Attitudes toward self and others determine effectiveness. Attitudes are the eyes of my soul through which I view the world, events, and people.

Have you ever asked yourself why in the church we so often overlook attitudes? Regrettably, dysfunctional or destructive attitudes are often disregarded in persons we recruit, in those we add to our ministry team, or in those we try to help develop. In spite of the fact that we know rotten attitudes create problems, we often ignore them. But to ignore or tolerate bad attitudes in staff members over time is to sabotage the ministries of a local congregation.

Have you ever asked yourself why in the church we so often overlook attitudes?

Harmful attitudes toward self are especially damaging. In an insightful article in *Time* magazine published several years ago, a Harvard psychiatrist interviewed successful people from contemporary professions who had failed terribly. The amazing but true-to-life thesis of his article was that most people cannot consistently rise above their own personal self-image.

For those in ministry with a poor self-image, this means the moment they have more success than their self-image thinks they deserve, they undermine themselves. Consider that dreadfully alarming possibility of committing unconscious subversion against yourself. If the idea is even partially true, it has incredible significance for those you develop in ministry.

All this suggests leaders do not rise higher than their self-image allows because they can't. It means my attitudes about myself determine how I perceive what others do. Thus, I cannot develop anyone more than my belief about myself and others allows. My friend Charles Swindoll is right: "Life is 10 percent what happens to me and 90 percent how I react to it."

Remember the two tracks we have been discussing for leaders. Attitudes must also move down those two tracks. That means harmful attitudes are always a thousand times more critical when the harmful attitude shows up in a leader near the top of an organization, like the senior pastor.

At the same time on the other track, attitudes must be considered a key factor in selecting staff members for your church's team. One person with destructive attitudes on any church team will sap a church's spiritual energy and undermine its growth.

It is also critically important in choosing staff members for you to thoroughly check out your own attitudes toward them even as you cautiously evaluate their attitudes toward ministry, you, their spouse, other people, and life in general.

2. Listen Carefully to Their Dreams

Great leaders have vision and know how to communicate vision so other people want to make it happen. That quality is important in members of your staff. Having a vision in itself, however, does not make a leader, though it is an important starting point. And though you may not realize it, as senior pastor you can nourish or crush a potential staff person's dream with a look, a nod, or a sentence.

Ask a potential staffer, "What is the most satisfying thing that could happen to you?" Then listen closely to the answer. He or she might reply something like this, "The most fulfilling thing for me is to have a dream, share it with the people I lead, and then for us to go to the mountain together to accomplish the vision." Dreams in pastors and staff members are where magnificent achievements begin.

> *ou can strongly believe in a vision but conclude the price is too high.*

As a leader of staff and volunteers, you should be aware that almost every vision passes through two valleys. First, after you see a vision clearly and start to think through its implications and possibilities, you go into a serious dip, a valley called ownership. The issue is simply this—you are trying to determine whether you are prepared to own the vision.

The second valley comes quickly—this valley is called price. What is the vision going to cost? You can strongly believe in a vision but conclude the price is too high. Every vision given to a leader has a price tag. Look at these biblical examples:

Abraham—Cost him a life of toil on difficult soil (Gen. 13:10-17).

Jacob—Cost him alienation from his family (Gen. 18:10-22), physical pain, and disability (32:22-32).

Joseph—Cost him rejection and alienation from his family (Gen. 37:12-36) and years of slavery and imprisonment (37:36; 39:1, 20).

David—Cost him the death of 70,000 Israelites (1 Chron. 21:14—22:1).

Solomon—Cost him his childhood (1 Chron. 22:5, 17; 29:1) and years of labor (2 Chron. 8:1).

Nehemiah—Cost him his job (Neh. 1:11).

Elisha—Cost him his source of income (1 Kings 19:20-21).

Peter—Cost him time, money, job (Luke 5:11) and imprisonment (Acts 12:5).

Paul—Cost him physical suffering, blindness (Acts 9:8); beating (14:19); starvation (27:33); and imprisonment (Acts 21:27).

Jesus—Cost Him His life.

3. Look for Relational People

All genuine leaders excel in happy, wholesome relationships. Excellent relationships among staff members are the raw materials of a happy, productive team. Look for staff personnel who love people and show it.

I saw a study on why people quit church that I never want to forget. Consider these percentages: 1 percent die, 3 percent move away, 5 percent follow new friendships, 9 percent move to competition, 14 percent become dissatisfied, and 68 percent quit because of an attitude of indifference toward them. Indifference shows in staff members or volunteers who do not relate well to people.

Let us remember relationships are highly significant and highly valued components in church life. Four relational realities between leaders and followers are always at work in a church:

- Happy relationships with other leaders give a leader influence.
- Satisfying relationships with followers build congregational stability.
- Caring relationships with new people give a leader a significant future.
- Excellent relationships with all groups give a leader respect across the congregation.

4. Put Yourself Under Evaluation.

An amazingly effective way to develop strong relationships with everyone in the church is for a pastor to initiate a voluntary evaluation of himself or herself by staff members and high-level lay leaders. Insisting that key people evaluate me helped me work on issues I had never realized or had ignored. The experience was humbling but helpful.

Of course, word got out through the staff, lay leaders, and key church members that I desired to be a growing person. The idea that I expected staff members to do the same was discussed through the congregation. This helped me in three significant ways: (1) I discovered my own serious blind spots, (2) I gained a reputation of wanting to be a growing person, and (3) improvement became the accepted norm in the congregation.

5. Challenge Staff Persons with the Rebekah Principle

Leaders on a church team, especially staff members, must commit to excellence. Let me underscore this idea: The highly effective staff person never allows himself or herself or anyone he or she supervises to give average performance. Giving get-by service is not in his or her leadership style.

Excellence derives from the word *excel,* which means to go beyond what is expected. Dale Carnegie taught, "Don't be afraid to give your best to what seems to be a small job. Every time you conquer one, it makes you that much stronger. If you do little jobs well, the big ones tend to take care of themselves."

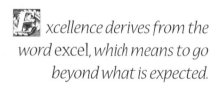

xcellence derives from the word excel, *which means to go beyond what is expected.*

Remember in the Old Testament how Abraham sent his servant to find a bride for Isaac. When Rebekah, the prospective bride, came down to the well, she asked, "Can I give you a drink of water?"

Then she added something that is important for our thinking about staff development: "And can I get your camels something to drink?" At first, her words seem like a kind gesture until we recall that Abraham's servant had 10 camels. Then we realize her offer was quite amazing. This caravan had traveled all day, and I am told that an average camel, after a day's journey, drinks 20 gallons of water. Think of the what she communicated when she offered, "Can I give your camels something to drink?"

She actually was saying, "I am willing to go back to that well, put my bucket down, and draw water until I have drawn enough water for 10 camels." That is 200 gallons of water—sounds like going well beyond the average call of duty.

Once I put a calculator to this event to try to understand what Rebekah offered. Think of it like this: If no one was standing in line for the well and every camel was close by, it would still take her perhaps 3 minutes to drop the bucket down and draw it back. If it was a 5-gallon bucket, it would take 40 trips and at 3 minutes each trip, you have a total of 2 hours. If my math is even close, Rebekah was a "willing to do whatever it takes" kind of person.

When she said, "Can I get your camels some water also?" she expressed a willingness to go to an extreme level of selfless service, well beyond anyone's expectations. I love to call this commitment the "Rebekah principle." It is a wonderful attitude to have in our own leadership and to encourage in the staff members we recruit and develop.

Of course, this Rebekah principle is contradictory to our contemporary culture's view of work, which expects to invest minimum effort for maximum expectations. Today's philosophy expects to give minimum effort for maximum benefit. But the Rebekah principle offers to serve with maximum effort for minimum benefit.

Prospective staff members who want guarantees, tenure, security, and perks remind me of star professional athletes. Have you ever considered how amazing it is that big-salaried athletes never think of going back to the ball club owner and offering, "I had a rotten year. Since I was overpaid for such poor performance, I want to return some of my salary." It has never happened yet in the history of baseball, basketball, or church.

The Rebekah principle, however, knows no grasping self-interest. It delivers on the "what can I give" way of life. She taught us how to say, "I am going to give the maximum effort for minimum expectation." Her types go the second mile and beyond.

The Christian community is filled with too many wimpy, no-effort, no-risk people. I agree 100 percent with my friend Zig Ziglar: "There is no traffic jam on the extra mile." Second milers, those who practice the Rebekah principle, make the best staff members who impact the most people for Christ.

STAFF LESSONS FROM SKYLINE

When I became pastor of Skyline Church in San Diego, I found a wonderful church that had enjoyed a long-term, happy relationship with a greatly loved senior pastor. Nonetheless, the church was in serious trouble because the staff team could not carry the church to greater growth and higher accomplishments.

At our first staff meeting, I drew a line across a marker board. I put 1,000 on the line—that is what the attendance had been running for 12 years. They had never averaged 1,100 for a year and seldom had they been under 1,000 even for a month. Then I put a big question mark above the 1,000 line.

Then I said kindly, "Let me tell you that I know this staff has the ability to lead 1,000 people. That is a proven fact. My question is, can this staff lead the church to 2,000?"

> *You can count on me to pour my ministry into you. I am going to help you grow and show you how to strengthen relationships.*

I continued with tough love: "I also know that under your present ways of doing ministry you do not have the ability to lead this church to 2,000. If this staff could do that, the attendance would be 2,000. So let us admit that the way this staff operates, leads, ministers, helps, prays, and serves, we cannot lead a congregation of 2,000."

Then I continued with a challenge: "I do not know if you have the potential inside you to lead the church to 2,000. But I want to find out. You can count on me to pour my ministry into you. I am going to help you grow and show you how to strengthen relationships. I am going to come alongside of you as your coach, your brother, your partner. My goal is to help you reach your full potential."

Then I explained the hardest part: "The only way this church can move from 1,000 to 2,000 is through an orderly process of change. The price between 1,000 and 2,000 is that every one of you is going to have to change in some way."

Here is the principle: If a church always does what it has always done, it will always get the results it has always gotten. That is the mode of operation in many contemporary churches. Such a mind-set says, "We have always done what we have always done and we will not change." Then the church wonders why the results are always the same.

Let me continue what I said to the Skyline staff: "My goal is for you to change. My goal is to help you in your area of responsibility to become a leader who can carry your part in a church of 2,000. But if I cannot change you or if you do not want to change, then you probably do not want to continue on this staff."

Let us make one point as clear as the sunrise. As pastor of a church entrusted to you by God, you are a steward of the human gifts and personal abilities in that part of the Body. That includes everyone in that congregation—yourself, staff, lay leaders, and church members. Just as we would not squander financial resources or mismanage facilities, human resources must not be wasted.

Let us face that fact that many Christian leaders do not want to make tough, emotional, and political decisions. Expediency, however, is dangerous in the kingdom of God—especially when you begin to think of all the people who could have been won for Christ while we were trying to keep from "rocking the boat."

Let me say it honestly. Some Christian leaders make a living out of lying. Some cannot tell the truth for a whole day when it comes to personnel issues. For the sake of sparing hurt feelings, they say things that are not true.

Do you have people you ought to be dealing with but don't? Do you have staff members you ought to insist improve? Do you have ministries that have reached a dead end because nobody is willing to speak truthfully concerning the key human hindrances? Of course, high prices have to be paid. But what about the not-so-obvious price of doing nothing?

Let us get a grip on our leadership so we are constantly evaluating personnel for effective Kingdom growth. Strengthen your backbone and do what you know has to be done.

7

LEADING VISIONARY LEADERS

Developing Leaders for the New Century

by Dale Galloway

A lifetime advocate of lay ministry, Elton Trueblood loved to say, "The laity are not the passengers of a ship. They are members of the crew." George Hunter's book *Church for the Unchurched* examines a number of today's breakthrough congregations from a wide range of denominations and locations. Though each church differed in style, they all valued laypeople in ministry. In short, churches that make a significant difference in people's lives find ways to release God's people to reach and serve others in Jesus' name.

Potential leaders must know they are trusted and empowered to do their ministry and to do it well. That takes doing in the church what this memorandum from U.S. President George Bush attempted to do in government: "Think big. Challenge the system. Adhere to the highest ethical standards. Be on the record as much as possible. Be frank. Fight hard for your position. When I make a call, we move as a team. Work with Congress. Represent the United States with dignity" (as quoted in Burt Nanus, *Visionary Leadership*). Encouragement and empowerment are what the potential lay leader needs from us. Building leaders depends on our trusting them.

On a personal and almost confessional note, God wants to mature us as leaders of leaders who enjoy seeing other people accomplish effective ministry. Whether it is leading someone to faith in Christ or visiting someone in the hospital, we can genuinely enjoy seeing the people of the congregation outshine us. Today I get bigger satisfaction from seeing others who are effectively using their spiritual gifts than from my own achievements. My vision for ministry must be bigger than my own limitations of talents, time, and perspective.

SEEK TO DEVELOP LEADERS MORE THAN FOLLOWERS

Though some pastors may desire to make followers, I seek to develop leaders. Not only do I want to make leaders, but I want to develop leaders of leaders. And then my next step is to develop leaders of leaders of leaders. Leadership can only be multiplied by developing leaders.

eadership can only be multiplied by developing leaders.

There are three leadership development levels that every pastor must understand and use. These levels are ideally developed simultaneously.

• **Know your own leadership.** The first is the development of your own leadership. That is a lifetime process. I am still trying to be a leader. Few potential or capable leaders are willing to follow so-called leaders who do not continually improve themselves. And growing your own leadership is satisfying, fulfilling work. But radical individual competence or dictatorial control will not build a church—we really do need others to help us.

• **Grow other leaders.** The second level is when other leaders are developed. It is here that you start to multiply your effectiveness and maximize your own abilities. If you have to be at the center of everything, your church cannot go further than you can reach.

If you do not grow secure enough in the Lord and in His love, you will not be free to let other people be themselves and grow into greatness. You cannot delight in others who are doing significant ministry if you are an insecure person. You will not trust them, and they will not be confident in stretching themselves. One of the most exciting days of my life was when I discovered four ministries in our church that I did not know we had, and I was the founding pastor. That was a great payoff after years and years of developing leaders and giving ministry to other people.

• **Grow other leaders who develop leaders.** The third and most productive level is when you become a leader of leaders who develop leaders. Lone Ranger type pastors or "do it myself" lay leaders never grow strong churches. The fundamental principle is this—God never gives us a vision we can fulfill by ourselves. When you get serious about reaching this level is when your church gets on an exponential curve of multiple blessing, achieving far more than you ever dreamed was possible.

God has never given me anything worthwhile to do that I could accomplish by myself.

God has never given me anything worthwhile to do that I could accomplish by myself. Every ministry vision has always required me to (1) stretch beyond where I was, (2) depend completely on God or it would not happen, and (3) recruit and mobilize others to help make the dream a reality. Meeting those requirements puts you at the exciting place where multiplication takes place.

As the number of trained lay pastors at New Hope Community Church grew, soon their combined reach and incredible achievement were far beyond what I could personally do. At any waking hour of any day, one or more groups were meeting, offering care one to another in Jesus' name.

THE JESUS PATTERN FOR LEADING LEADERS

Lately I have been thinking about how Jesus was such an exemplary leader of leaders. An insightful book, *The Leadership Lessons of Jesus,* has been helping me think seriously and frequently about the caring connections our Lord had with His disciples. After discussing Mark 3:35, "Whatever does God's will is my brother and sister and mother," authors Briner and Pritchard remind us of leaders' obligations to those they lead. They observe, "Jesus, the greatest of all leaders, clearly represents the special relationship that can evolve between leaders and followers. He never exhibited a cool detachment toward them; they were not simply pawns to carry out His wishes and implement His plans. His followers were very special to Him, and, conversely, He was very special to them." Leading leaders starts with loving them, cherishing them, and trusting them. It involves taking them into our hearts and teaching them to do what we know to do.

There is also the important dimension of shared ministry and vision. Briner and Pritchard explain, "This mutual caring, mutually productive, mutually protective, nonexploitive leader/follower relationship that Jesus maintained with His disciples is a model for all leaders and followers." Shared ministry brings leaders and potential leaders together in indescribably fulfilling ways. I sometimes wonder who receives the greatest good—the leader or the leaders who are being developed.

IMPLEMENTING CHANGES IN THE WAY WE DO MINISTRY

I was teaching a class last year with our Beeson pastors when I said, "In developing a church from 0 to 6,300 members, at every point of progress I had to change before we could move to the next level in our growth."

It is only by examining and reexamining your opinions and ideas that you can progress."

A sharp student asked, "How did you have to change?" Though I had never thought that through, I was aware there were certain points where I changed the way I used my time and how I did ministry. Dale Carnegie's advice quoted in *The Leader in You* (Levine/Crom) works well in those who wish to develop leaders: "Keep your mind open to change all the time. Welcome it. Court it. It is only by examining and reexamining your opinions and ideas that you can progress."

My ideas about these changes were clarified a few months ago when I discovered a new book by Alan Nelson called *Leading Your Ministry*. He breaks our task into three categories—ministry, managing, and leadership. As I interacted with Nelson's book, I wrote down all the things we do that fit these three categories. Here are my lists:

Ministry
- Preaching
- Prayer
- Care and counseling
- Sacraments
- Evangelism
- Weddings and funerals
- Teaching
- Discipleship
- Hospital calling

Management
- Building
- Personnel
- Insurance
- Decision meetings
- Programs
- Daily operations
- Finances
- Policy
- Denominational responsibility

Leadership
- Vision casting
- Focus/refocus
- Training
- Planning
- Recruiting
- Practicing Jethro Principle
- Mentoring
- Small groups
- Influencing influencers
- Team building
- Networking
- Restrictive problems
- Implementation
- Problem solving
- Teaching/modeling ministry
- Communication
- Time with God

- Training leaders to lead leaders
- Delegates
- Empowers
- Understands culture
- Sees it before others
- Responsible for the church's effectiveness

Because 90 percent of all pastors spend their whole life alone in ministry, they seldom are challenged to become proficient at the management or leadership levels. That is why they do not know how to pastor a church bigger than 100 people. Should they try, they might have a nervous breakdown because they feel they have to do everything themselves. But face this indisputable fact—you never grow a church to an attendance of 250 until you learn how to manage. And to grow a large church, you must learn how to be a leader of leaders. Try applying Allen Nelson's categories to your situation:

- **Ministry.** We all start out doing sacraments, teaching, preaching, and counseling. We also do weddings and offer pastoral care. Most of our training in college and seminary has to do with this one-person ministry.

- **Management.** Now look at this next area. Under managing, I wrote down my list. Here you have board meetings, budgets, personnel, organization, and institutional strengthening. Now, if you are going to grow a church, you have to begin sharing responsibility in this area.

- **Leadership.** In this category, I listed most of what I did as a senior pastor of New Hope Community Church when we grew to 6,000 members. Here is how I spent my time—vision, vision casting, leadership development, training, planning, staffing, influencing influencers, mentoring, small groups, team building, spotting growth-restrictive problems and solving them. Then I added networking, problem solving, teaching ministry while modeling it, practicing good communication, training leaders to lead leaders, spending time with God. As you can see, the list is very subjective and shows a lot about how I work and think. The list got pretty long, but for our purposes it is important to notice how different it is from the first list of ministry.

Let's think of the ways ministry expands and changes from

one category to the next. In the first list when I started in ministry, I just did preaching—sometimes without a specific focus or aim. But as the church grew, I preached for a purpose so I could lead the congregation to where we were going. So I did series preaching because the purpose now behind what I preached was to lead through modeling and sharing ministry: share with others, delegate, and empower. Now in addition to having a message for the entire congregation, I was also demonstrating ministry for leaders I was developing.

> *You have to question your perspective, ask yourself to rethink your strategies of ministry, and adjust the way you work.*

The underlying reality is this—the only way you can grow a larger healthy church is to change how you do ministry well before the church changes. You have to question your perspective, ask yourself to rethink your strategies of ministry, and adjust the way you work. That is the amazing adventure and joy of growing a church. You are forced to grow with it. And when you stop growing, the church generally stops growing. You will never move to the next stage of growth and congregational health unless you intentionally change how you do ministry.

The transition time from spending most of your time in ministry to spending more time in the leadership category may be among the most challenging adjustments of your ministry pilgrimage. During this transition, you will be working like you have two jobs. For example, you will be doing ministry much like you always have while at the same time recruiting, training, motivating, and beginning to get other people doing ministry.

In this process of change, be aware of one all-important reality that is increasingly being neglected in larger churches. A senior pastor, regardless of his leadership tasks, always teaches by modeling ministry. Thus, there is never a time when the senior pastor moves away from actually doing hands-on ministry. Though I did ministry differently, I kept doing ministry. Thus, I had a neighbor next door to whom I witnessed. I brought new people into small groups I led. I raised leaders up out of that small group to start the next group. But to grow a healthy church, I must recognize that my span of care is only about 10 or 15 people, and if I try to care for more people than that, I am in difficulty. But for both the church and my own sense of ministerial fulfillment, I must do some hands-on ministry. Thus, in a larger church, when I stand up and put my arm around someone and say, "I love you and it was such a joy to pray with you," the whole congregation knows I actually do ministry.

If you, however, decide to move completely away from doing ministry yourself, you will end up merely running a human organization. I doubt if that is satisfying ministry. For me, I need ministry, even with a few people, to keep authentic and focused. And so do you. Among the most significant ministry tasks of a visionary leader is to be a pastor to the staff, decision makers, and influencers. But they are the ones who actually multiply ministry.

These changes, however, are sometimes difficult to implement. A lady I pastored some 28 years ago wrote me: "My husband was in the hospital. He had a surgery and you did not come see him. I have held this grudge against you all these years. I do not think I am going to live long. Would you please forgive me so I can go to heaven?" I wrote back and apologized, "I am sorry I let you down."

Let's remember this lady is typical of a lot of people in our churches. I gave that level of care to a certain group in the church—the board, the staff, and my neighbors—because I needed to model ministry to teach it. Therefore, since I had a limited span of care; I could only reach so far. To reach farther beyond what I could do, I had to touch people through other people. The trick is not to abandon or curtail ministry but to expand it through empowering and training others.

Here is an important discovery we made. As New Hope Church grew, we learned people who came into the fellowship through small groups looked to their small groups for pastoral care. People who came in through the ministry of other staff members looked to them for their pastoral care; they did not look to me. But I still had people I cared for even though I was senior pastor of this large church.

Three issues are critical to becoming a leader of leaders: (1) every pastor has to do some one-to-one ministry in order to be personally fulfilled and in order to model ministry; (2) everyone needs pastoral care from someone; (3) those who received pastoral care from the pastor when the church was smaller may always expect and need it from the senior minister.

> *our vision for ministry has to be bigger than your desire to be the personal pastoral caregiver for everyone.*

In growing a church, you have to change by moving the time you spend from category one (ministry) to two (management) to three (leadership). Now, if you visit great growing churches, you will find those pastors spend the majority of their time in category number three—leadership. That is the only way they can do it. It is also true for you.

Your vision for ministry has to be bigger than your desire to be the personal pastoral caregiver for everyone. Your personal reach is too tiny compared to all the needs that should be touched.

When the pastor continues as the primary caregiver, the ministry will always be limited. It is interesting that while we think we are working ourselves to death for the glory of God, we really limit the work of God when we try to do it all by ourselves. What an amazing discovery about ourselves and about ministry.

LEARNING FROM MOSES' MENTOR

Consider the account in Exod. 18:13-27 where Moses was trying to do it all. Moses' father-in-law, Jethro, said to him, "What you are doing is not good . . . The work is too heavy for you; you cannot handle it alone" (Exod. 18:17-18).

Do you see the picture clearly?—3 million people who were lined up every day for as far as you can see. They came early in the morning and stayed until late at night. They thought they had to see Moses, and they were frustrated by the fact of his unavailability.

Like a lot of us, Moses' ego loved it when people "come to me to seek God's will" (v. 15). But Moses was his own worst enemy. He was killing himself physically and emotionally with his good but mistaken intentions. He was overworked and cripplingly stressed. What could he do?

Jethro carefully looked over this situation and observed, "Moses, this is not right for you or the people." If he were among us today, he might say, "You are in codependency; this is sick." Sometimes we ministers get a sick enjoyment from what we are doing but do not know how to change. Or maybe we do not want to change.

In this biblical passage from Exodus, we see three problems that are still with us in the church today.

• **Burnout.** It sneaks up on us as we do five things. Then someone says let's do something more. You agree and now you are doing six, soon seven, and then eight, and then nine. But how much can you do? How much time do you have? And have you ever been able to add a day to your week?

Let's work with a reality that can free us: A leader is not someone who does the work of 10 people. Rather, a real leader is someone who gets 10 people to do the work of 10 people. Or, a leader is someone who gets 100 people to do the work of 100 people. Or, a leader is someone who gets 1,000 people to do the work of 1,000 people.

You must learn how to peel off some activities. Talk to yourself until you are convinced that every time you successfully delegate some task, you will eventually be freed up with more time to invest in something else. For 15 years I thought that the harder I worked and the longer I worked, the better I was as a minister. I was sadly mistaken.

What is wrong with such a notion of hard work? Of course, I believe pastors should work hard. But when carried to the extreme, you are headed for burnout. In such a mode, your life is out of balance. You are not a good marriage partner or parent. And in the process, you limit what other people can do.

• **Dissatisfaction.** A high level of dissatisfaction among the congregation is the second problem. Now every church has some level of dissatisfaction. Someone will always be dissatisfied, and that someone is frequently changing. For many years, I thought it was my job as a pastor to keep everyone happy. When I first started, we had congregational votes every year, so it was imperative to keep everybody happy. But often such a goal is a no-win situation because people decide whether or not they are going to be happy.

The key question as you evaluate satisfaction at your church should be: "Is the church focused on effectively serving people in the name of Jesus?"

o what Moses did. Get people
mobilized. Raise up leaders.

All dissatisfaction must carefully be considered, however. Too many pastors dismiss dissatisfaction as coming from unreasonable critics. Many times the dissatisfaction, however, is warranted because it is rooted in unmet needs or poor organization of ministry in a church. Sometimes we have a real problem that is creating unrest, and we raise satisfaction by giving attention to solving the difficulty. That is how it was for Moses.

So a pastor might ask himself and trusted lay leaders, "How can I improve the satisfaction level?" Do what Moses did. Get people mobilized. Raise up leaders. Appoint a leader over 10, then appoint a leader over those 10. As people get involved in ministry where they are using their spiritual gifts, they discover incredible satisfaction and enjoy amazing fulfillment.

At New Hope Community Church, we had 550 lay pastors. When those lay leaders came to church, they were motivated and charged up. So were the people they were caring for.

Here is an absolutely dependable principle: There is a direct ratio between the satisfaction level and people involvement in ministry. The biblical pattern for satisfaction and achievement comes from Jethro's directive to Moses: "Select capable men from all the people—men who fear God, trustworthy men who hate dishonest gain—and appoint them as officials over thousands, hundreds, fifties and tens. . . . If you do this and God so commands, you will be able to stand the strain, and all these people will go home satisfied" (18:21, 23). That is the way to increase satisfaction—get more people involved actually doing ministry.

• **Unhealthy self-reliance.** Moses believed like some of us that no one can do the work as well as we can. The notion is silly as well as false. A friend of mine pastors a church of 150. He started the church and continued doing everything himself for many years. Then he added his first associate. Soon after that, I stopped by his church on my way to having lunch with him. I waited. I waited. I waited. People kept going in and out of my friend's office. There was a holy bustle about the place. So I walked down the hallway to use up a little time. I looked through the window of an adjoining office where the new associate had his feet on the desk, watching the ball game on TV, and drinking a Coke. I noticed, too, that he had his golf clubs all shined up for the afternoon. When my friend finally got free, I said, "You have added a new associate."

"Oh," he said, "he's a fine young man."

I asked, "What does he do?"

He scratched his head and he said, "Well, I've been trying to come up with something."

We all laugh, but is my friend different from many of us? We think everybody has to be dependent on us. But we limit our ministry until we break out of this self-imposed prison. We box in our ministry until we give some of it away. Only what we share in ministry multiplies.

There is a key word that sums up this teaching in Exod. 18. Though *delegate* obviously summarizes this passage, my favorite words for this passage are *release* and *empower*. I love *empower* because it means to decentralize. It means that when a new person comes to your church, you hand the visitor's card to one of your small-group leaders, who follows up. The ideal is to get ministry down as close to the front line as possible.

Now, I worked so effectively at decentralizing ministry that one day I realized my strength was starting to become a little weakness. Let me explain. I had 15 district pastors. They had their small groups, their lay pastors, and their district. Everything was working like clockwork. Then I woke up to realize the church was starting to lose the vision. Not me. But the vision was not coming through the lay leaders to members of their small groups. That is when I learned you cannot delegate the vision. No matter how large the church gets, you still have to spend time with key staff people and influential influencers to keep the vision fresh for yourself, for them, and for the whole congregation.

The bottom line of Moses' following the advice of Jethro—he could do more in less time through other people (18:13-27).

MOSES, TEACH US HOW TO
EMPOWER AND DECENTRALIZE

Moses did six things after he heard Jethro's tough-love warning (18:18-19). He recruited, he trained, he organized, he set up a chain of commands, he delegated, and that made it possible for him to balance his life. What a relevant passage of Scripture for contemporary pastors.

*eal leaders look hard for real
people with real virtues."*

• **He recruited.** Briner and Pritchard, in *The Leadership Lessons of Jesus,* offer this compelling advice: "Jesus' example in recruiting effective followers suggests that we cast the widest possible net. Consider everyone on his or her merit. Accept talent, character, and commitment where you find it . . . Real leaders look hard for real people with real virtues. Jesus showed how spectacularly successful a leader can be with carefully chosen followers from all walks of life." Perhaps the final measurement of ministry in the sight of God is how much we helped others accomplish in Kingdom efforts.

• **He trained.** Too often our ideas about training and development are too schoolish—that is, we think we have to have classes and textbooks and lectures in order to train people for Kingdom service. In this passage, Moses trains the people by asking them to try. So much of their training was on-the-job training.

Laurie Beth Jones in *Jesus CEO: Using Ancient Wisdom for Visionary Leadership* helps solidify our ideas about training when she says of Jesus, "He kept teaching and sharing and demonstrating his ministry so team members would learn that they, too, had the power and ability to do what he had done."

Jethro was right to tell Moses, "Teach them the decrees and

laws, and show them the way to live and the duties they are to perform" (v. 20). And he also gave Moses two necessary qualities of leadership that the ones who are to be chosen must have: "trustworthy men who hate dishonest gain" (v. 21).

• **He organized.** Moses organized them to accomplish ministry. The passage says, "He [Moses] chose capable men from all Israel and made them officials over thousands, hundreds, fifties and tens" (v. 25). So much of what is called overwork in the church is merely disorganization.

• **He delegated.** People learn ministry by doing ministry. I was back in Columbus, Ohio, recently where I preached my first sermon at 17 years of age. I preached the whole Bible through in 15 minutes. But I started learning to preach that day by doing it.

What makes you hold back? Have you ever said, "They cannot do it as well as I can"? But how do people learn? You must allow them to try even when they make mistakes. Or how many have ever said, "It is just faster to do it myself"? Of course it takes more time up front, but it saves time later. The management specialist Michael Korda (quoted in Alan Loy McGinnis, *The Balanced Life*) is right: "Delegation is half of success. People who cannot delegate will find themselves fatally handicapped."

• **He balanced his life.** Jethro advised that shared ministry would "make your [Moses'] load lighter, because they will share it with you. If you do this and God so commands, you will be able to stand the strain, and all these people will go home satisfied" (vv. 22-23). Balance for Moses came when he listened to a trusted confidant, when he shared ministry, when he kept from delegating only what he could do, and when he gave ownership of the work to others so they did the work and ceased their complaints.

Look at the results Moses achieved. New leaders felt fulfilled because they were using their spiritual gifts. He became a healthy leader. The people were satisfied because they were now useful, cared for, and needed.

WHAT DRAWS POTENTIAL LEADERS TO LEADERSHIP ASSIGNMENTS

In the church, we always start with the motivation of service for our Lord. People serve also because they are needed or because some think they can do it. William N. Yeomans, in *1000 Things You Never Learned in Business School,* provides this list of ways to help them give their best effort:

1. Let them know what's expected.
2. Keep them informed.
3. Give them control.
4. Give them start-to finish responsibility.
5. Make them champions.
6. Give them feedback.
7. Give them appreciation.
8. Help them learn and grow.
9. Be approachable.

n the church, we always start with the motivation of service for our Lord.

MY DISCOVERY ABOUT BECOMING A LEADER OF LEADERS

For me, the motivation to delegate was to accomplish the vision and dream of our church. Without the help of other people, I could not fulfill my calling to reach the unchurched thousands in Portland, Oregon. When the vision is bigger than anything that holds you back, it will drive you beyond your reluctance to delegate.

My biggest regret in 23 years of ministry in Portland is that we did not delegate more. Some pastors want to make followers. I want to make leaders—to develop other people and release their giftedness. Look across your church and ask if God would have you do the same in your assignment.

⁘ 8 ⁘

VISIONARY LEADERS ENCOUNTER GREATNESS

A Consuming Passion for Kingdom Usefulness

by Elmer Towns

Years ago, I gave a lecture series titled "Encounter with Greatness" at Owosso College (Michigan), later renamed John Wesley College. Since the school was having financial difficulties, I was given a beautiful bust of John Wesley in place of an honorarium. I still have that bust in my office where it reminds me to read and think about John Wesley. Every contact with Wesley is an encounter with greatness. Wesley fits one of my favorite descriptions of a great leader. Really great leaders stop disasters, capture kingdoms, build empires, and influence people in the deepest part of their life.

Consider the strengths that many great leaders possess: They have a task that consumes them, irrepressible passion, uncanny insight, abandonment to the task, and above-average intelligence.

In that "Encounter with Greatness" series, I tried to share what I have discovered about great leaders, and I have thought a lot about it since then. Vibrant Christians who build great, strong, healthy churches carefully follow the directive of Jesus: "Do you want to stand out? Then step down. Be a servant. If you puff yourself up, you'll get the wind knocked out of you. But if you're content to simply be yourself, your life will count for plenty" (Matt. 23:11-12, TM).

Authentic greatness is an important issue for pastors because I am convinced that only great people build great, healthy churches.

> *R eally great leaders stop*
> *disasters, capture kingdoms,*
> *build empires, and influence*
> *people in the deepest part*
> *of their life.*

Think about what genuine greatness really is. Consider our Lord's scathing criticism of the Pharisees and how that applies to contemporary ministers: "Be careful about following *them.* They talk a good line, but they don't live it. They don't take it into their hearts and live it out in their behavior. It's all spit-and-polish veneer" (Matt. 23:3, TM). That is not greatness even though they were religious, brilliant, and talkative.

A great leader is a person of Christlike character, an individual to be thoroughly trusted. He gives wholehearted attention to vision, reality, ethics, courage, and Kingdom values. Greatness involves more than measurable achievement—it starts with the leader's heart and not his or her head. It is rooted in virtues like self-sacrifice, love, courage, loyalty, accountability, humility, meaning, mission, passion, and commitment.

George Barna, in his book *The Power of Vision,* sorts out the greatness issue for me with three sentences: "In our own century, there are numerous examples of people who, by human standards, showed little promise for greatness and little hope of being able to change the lives of people around the world. But these people, having captured God's vision for ministry, have lived with power and energy that undeniably transcend their natural capacities and with an intensity of commitment that far exceeds anything they had previously demonstrated in their lives. The results of their efforts further expose the power of God at work within them."

Everyone realizes, of course, that a pastor with a growing church has to have unusual ability, or even a creative mentality, to pull in increasing numbers. But great churches are not just churches with impressive crowds. Many influential churches have an inspiring missionary heart and give money and people to missions. Many highly visible churches have an impressive commitment to training young people for Christian service. Other influential congregations are in the church-planting business. Meanwhile, certain other churches are evangelistic churches. All these highly visible churches do a variety of significant work and

 *reat churches start with great leaders.*

accomplish many worthwhile achievements. But do these qualities and activities make a church great? Not by themselves. There is something more. Though each of these ministries has its place, a church can never be great in service to Christ and genuinely effective in ministry that is not led by a great leader. Great churches start with great leaders.

How, then, is greatness defined and developed? How is greatness measured?

All the great influential pastoral leaders I have studied have a consuming cause to which they give high commitment in time, thought, values, and energies. They are driven by a cause that dominates all they are and all they think. Their vision impacts and prioritizes everything else. These pastors are incredibly focused on what they consider to be significant. And they constantly think and talk about developing a church that will revolutionize people's lives.

Though he was writing to secular leaders, Peter Koestenbaum helps us understand greatness in his book *Leadership: The Inner Side of Greatness* when he writes: "Greatness is not sought because it furthers other values. It is not an instrumental good. Greatness is an intrinsic value, an inherent good, a pure virtue. It is good in and of itself. It is to be sought for its own sake. It is chosen as a way of life because it is right, because it ennobles the human spirit, because it honors the fact that we are alive, and because it is our meaning for being on this earth." Later he says:

Greatness means to
- honor life by striving for depth and for perfection

and by devoting yourself to what is worthy and noble. . . .

- stand up to death and evil.
- be humble. Be open-minded. Understand the magni-
  tude of self-deception, and identify your resistances
  to authenticity.

When I observed effective church growth pastors around the
globe, I came to the conclusion that greatness in churches outside
America usually comes down to the miraculous ingredient called
faith connected with a consuming passion to accomplish a worthwhile cause. These pastors have something more than just skills
they have learned. These pastors, each in his or her own unique
way, are committed to help a person to become more Christlike.
They realize that you must become something before you do
something.

Although experience and ability are important, I know people who have impressive leadership skills who cannot lead an

> *Greatness starts with
> a personal journey with
> Christ within the individual.*

authentic growing community of believers in healthy spiritual
development. To achieve that, the truly great pastor must become something magnificent for God. Greatness starts with a
personal journey with Christ within the individual.

Bill Munroe is an impressive example. He was sitting in a
Baptist church in Indianapolis where he played the piano. With
a business degree from the University of South Carolina, Bill
was happy in his job and enjoyed being an active layman in his
church. But as he looked at the altar one Sunday morning where
12 people were kneeling, he thought, "I don't know of a church
in South Carolina where 12 people are being saved today." He
later reported, "At that moment, I was gripped as never before
or since with the call of God. I felt, just as Abraham, God say,
'Go to Chaldea.' I felt God say, 'Go,' and I was so convicted and
compelled, I resigned my job the next morning, put everything
I owned on a Ryder rental truck as soon as I could, and started

for South Carolina. God had called me to build a great church there.

"Halfway to South Carolina," he said, "I stopped the truck at a rest stop. As my wife, pregnant at the time, was stretching her back, I sat eating a sandwich on a concrete picnic table. Then she said, 'Bill, you don't know anything about planting a church or pastoring a church. Tell me, what kind of church can you build?'"

He said, "I took a napkin out of the picnic basket and wrote a five-year plan."

He started with the phrase "I'm going to build a church" and then made a list of specifics. "Number one was soul winning; I'm going to win people to the Lord." Then he thought for a moment and wrote number two, "Bible teaching; I'm going to teach the Bible." With that narrow vision that day, he went to South Carolina to build a church.

But he told his wife before they left the picnic table that day, "Honey, I can see it. I can see 10 acres of property with a big oak tree covered with Spanish moss. I can see southern pine trees. I can see a big yellow brick building with junipers growing up around the foundation."

He continued, "I can see a square auditorium with bright red carpet, padded pews, and in the square corner, up tall, there is going to be a pulpit. There will be a thousand people listening to me preach. Back of that, I'm going to put a large choir. And way up high, I'm going to put the baptistery."

With that clear vision, he went to Florence, South Carolina, to start a new church. He did not have a clue on how to plant a church. But he got a name tag that said "Bill Munroe, Pastor, Florence Baptist Temple." He went to K-Mart with 500 flyers that said, "Come hear me preach. Come hear me preach. Come hear me preach." And that first Saturday night, he got down to prepare his sermon. Then it dawned on him that he had never preached in his whole life.

Then in our conversation I asked him, "Bill, what in the world did you do?"

He replied, "I had taught Sunday School all my life, so I prepared a Sunday School lesson and got up and shouted it."

About four years later, I went to the church. As I drove south on 301, I saw 10 acres of ground. There was the live oak tree with Spanish moss. There were southern pine trees, a yellow brick square auditorium. Inside they had red carpet, red pews, an impressive pulpit, and a thousand people listening to him preach. He saw it and he did it. No one can achieve what they cannot conceive.

> *People of greatness have an incredible grip—a drive to achieve—within them.*

People of greatness have an incredible grip—a drive to achieve—within them. Notice this irrepressible urge in my friend Bill. He had this inner conviction that he was going to grow a church. He willingly abandoned everything else to accomplish the task.

Later, he reported, "For the first three months, I didn't have money. I didn't know how to get money. I charged everything on my Visa. Then when we reached our limit and couldn't charge any more, we started on our Sears card—but they don't have groceries there."

Then he said, "When I got right to the edge of desperate need, another pastor saw what I was doing and said, 'I want to help you financially.' It came in the nick of time."

Today, the church has 1,700 in Sunday School and 2,000 in worship; it is a strong church.

Bill Munroe is an impressive example of how a leader becomes great by allowing a consuming commitment to Christ to shape his vision and energize his efforts.

WHAT DO WE KNOW ABOUT GREATNESS IN LEADERS?

A good place to start to answer this question is to ask yourself or groups you lead to form an opinion poll of great leaders. You will make some amazing discoveries as you ask these questions of yourself and decision groups you work with:

1. Who is the most recognizable person in the world?
2. Who has influenced more people in this century than any other?

3. What Christian has had the greatest influence since Paul?

4. What Christian woman has had the greatest influence in this century?

5. What Christian man has had the greatest influence in this century?

6. Who has had the deepest influence on the greatest number of people in all history?

Here are a series of responses from my classes and conferences. Though you may come up with a different list, the process of working through the list of questions will clarify your group's concepts of greatness.

Who is the most recognizable person in the world? Colonel Sanders is the answer to the first question because his face is all over the world in Kentucky Fried Chicken advertising. He has face and name recognition, because marketing experts can sell chicken, but he has very little impact on what really counts. Recognition is not the same as influence—a reality Christian leaders must understand and cherish.

Who has influenced more people in this century than any other leader? Who would you say? Hitler? Billy Graham? Gandhi? Mao? For me it is Mao Tse-tung with his little red book, *Sayings of Mao.* He's influenced the largest nation in the world.

One of my students recently was reporting on research concerning the explosive growth of house churches throughout China. The student made the interesting conclusion that Mao was among the greatest influencers because when he controlled China, he organized the people into small groups. He taught the Chinese to read the same dialect and taught them to learn in groups. This counterculture unintentionally helped develop Christianity with its methodologies. Our lesson—often outside methods and ideas can be used in the service of God.

Turn now to question three: *What Christian has had the greatest influence since Paul?* If you are a Methodist, you will say John Wesley. If you are a Presbyterian, you will say John Calvin. If you are a Lutheran, you will say Martin Luther. My personal answer is John Wesley.

Question four, *What Christian woman has had the greatest*

impact in this century? You might say Mother Teresa, or Corrie ten Boom. I put Henrietta Mears first because of her incredible influence. Do you remember her story? She taught junior high school math in Minneapolis where she was a member of the First Baptist Church. She took winter vacations in California where she visited Hollywood Presbyterian Church and the pastor said, "Why don't you become my education director?" She accepted the challenge and started with a Sunday School of about 175. She built the Sunday School to about 4,000. One day, Bill

She wanted to have a revival meeting, and the elders of the church were against it.

Bright knocked on her door and said, "Someone told me that you should mentor me," and Bill Bright lived in her home for 10 years. Every morning at breakfast table, she discipled him, and he began Campus Crusade in her dining room.

She had a Sunday School class of about 400 and even won Hollywood stars to Jesus Christ. Dawson Trotman, Richard Halverson, and Bob Pierce were in her class. Thirty evangelical leaders came out of her Sunday School class. She worked from 5:00 to 8:00 every morning for years to write Gospel Light Sunday School literature.

She wanted to have a revival meeting, and the elders of the church were against it. So she took money out of her own pocket and rented a Mennonite tent, which she had set up at the county fair. She invited the president of a Bible college in her hometown to come hold the revival meeting. That Bible college was called Northwestern School—I'm a graduate of that school. And Billy Graham was the president. Graham was put on the map in the Los Angeles crusade as far as national recognition is concerned.

I would say she is the most influential Christian woman in this century because of her impact on young evangelical leaders.

What Christian man has had the greatest influence in this century? I think the greatest Christian leader in this century is Martin Luther King Jr. because he has influenced every American who has a job by initiating the Civil Rights Movement. He has influenced our society from sidewalk curb cuts to handicapped parking to feminists and to every minority. King has influenced us all. If I were to put the five greatest sermons preached since Pentecost, his "dream" sermon would be one of those five because of its profound impact.

Who has had the greatest influence on the greatest number of people in all history? Who has been the subject of more of the greatest books that have blessed the most people? Who has influenced the great music that has blessed the most people? Who has influenced building the most institutions that have been the greatest good for the most amount of people? Who is the one person who has affected more people? It is the Lord Jesus Christ. And He is our most obvious example of greatness.

WHAT DOES IT TAKE TO BE A GREAT LEADER?

An insightful dissertation by Ann Millner and Dorothy Millner, *The Rise and Role of Charismatic Leaders* (1965), deals with the personality traits of leaders in the military and politics. As I studied more than 20 doctoral dissertations discussing charismatic leadership, their study really stood out. Their study of leadership in politics and in the military has many significant things to say to pastors. They identified eight qualities:

• **Energy.** Persons who are great leaders have high levels of energy or extraordinary vitality. Winston Churchill could get by on three hours of sleep night after night as he led his country to wage war against Hitler. Peter Koestenbaum's sentence stretches the soul: "The energy we can summon—from sheer free will, self-discipline, determination, resoluteness, or guts—appears to be inexhaustible."

• **Cool head.** Persons who are great leaders possess unusual presence of mind under conditions of stress and challenge. They have the ability to control themselves, to know themselves, and to operate within themselves, but at the same time the ability to lift others to a high degree of attainment. Bob Briner and Ray Pritchard, in their book *The Leadership Lessons of Jesus*, remind us that "we need to *lead* through adverse circumstances, not be overcome by them. Nothing will raise a leader in the eyes of his or her followers more than when he or she effectively handles a crisis. Calm, effective leadership in the midst of a storm will do more to establish a leader than most any situation."

• **Decision maker.** Persons who are great leaders are strong-willed and firm in decision making. They make decisions work. They make decisions easily because they know where they

> *Persons who are great leaders are strong-willed and firm in decision making.*

want to go. They are willing to pay the price to get where they want to go. In his book *1000 Things You Never Learned in Business School,* William N. Yeomans advises, "Sometimes when you have made your decision, it is good to test it before you let it out of the cage. You can do that by taking the opposite view and thinking up all the arguments you can against it. If you can't think of too many strong ones, you probably have yourself a good decision."

• **Information synthesizer.** The great leader has mental ability to seize and use information from a wide variety of sources. As I interview great church leaders, I have noticed how many have an incredible amount of knowledge. They know, they see, they remember, they connect concepts, and they use information they have gathered both formally and informally from many people and places. These leaders are knowledgeable in the way they use what they know for the advancement of what they want to build for God.

• **Originality.** A person who is a strong leader has a flair for originality and a capacity for innovation. Years ago, I wrote a book called *A Christian Hall of Fame.* I was inspired for that writing project by Canton (Ohio) Baptist Temple where they had 108 pictures and drawings of Christian greats hanging in the halls of their church. As background for the book, I set out to find the best paragraph from each leader that summarized their perspective and drive. It took me about six months with the help of a graduate assistant who went through their writings and photocopied key paragraphs for me. Then I would read those quotes on airplanes, in airports, and in motels.

When I came to the end of my study of Christian leaders from the apostolic church fathers until now, I realized that each one stood above his contemporaries because he found his own niche and used a unique plan to accomplish ministry. And all were persons of great devotion. With John Wesley, it was called Methodism because he had new methods of doing ministry. Finney used new strategies that were criticized, but he was a powerful leader who fueled the Second Great Awakening. Go through church history and the pattern keeps reappearing.

Jerry Falwell uses innovative methods. Bill Hybels has a high name recognition and is influential because he found an original method called "seeker services" that he makes work. Rick Warren is another contemporary model. All of these ministry leaders are revered because people follow them, and others are making their methods work in many other settings.

• **Lack of economic fear.** A strong leader often has naïveté in financial matters. Of course, this strength can easily become a weakness. I do not recommend such naïveté, but I do believe in taking risks for God's kingdom. Faith always requires more than we can count in dollars and cents. Waiting for the perfect time and the ideal sum of money is a great excuse to stay stuck where you are. No great church's story can be told without many accounts of financial miracles, miracles that would not have happened without courageous risk and dependant faith.

• **Resourced by women.** A strong leader, male or female, often has ability to elicit an extraordinary degree of commitment from women. Many male church leaders are married to strong, capable women who either share the ministry in specific ways or provide behind-the-scenes encouragement and support. Women also make up a large part of the economic strength and workforce of most churches and para-church organizations.

Management specialist Laurie Beth Jones provides refreshing insight on the role of women: "Men who fail to acknowledge and enlist feminine energy often suffer for their arrogance. Pontius Pilate's wife, for example, tried to warn him not to be involved in the trial of Jesus. 'I had a dream about him,' she said (Matt. 27:19). Pilate ignored her and signed Jesus' death warrant, and his own unenviable place in history." She continues, "One comedienne theorized that perhaps the reason the Israelites wandered in the wilderness for forty years was because Moses wouldn't give Miriam the map."

In addition to the Millner studies, several other characteristics should be added to the list.

● **Guides through unstable environments.** A person who is a strong leader knows what to do with troubling or confusing situations. That means a change agent leader often arises during an unstable social milieu or frightening difficulties in the church. When people do not know what to do, they are often more willing to follow someone who stands up and says, "I can help you. Let's go this way." So as a church leader, when people are fearful, you must step forward and say, "I have the answer, and here is how we can make it work." Many clergy and lay leaders are clueless during rapid change, economic confusion, or generational torch passing. That is when new leaders often emerge.

s I look at great pastors, I ask why people follow them.

● **Propose specific plans for progress.** A person who is a strong leader devises a special formula for effectiveness. This is the phase where a leader proposes specific strategies or unique methodology. Charles Fuller used radio, and with a microphone he reached thousands. Robert Schuller did it with TV. D. James Kennedy did it with Evangelism Explosion. Bill Bright impacted thousands, maybe millions, when he said, "I have a new thing called the Four Spiritual Laws."

● **Demonstrates success.** A person who is a strong leader has a past basis of success on which to guarantee future success. As I look at great pastors, I ask why people follow them. I wonder what they do that you can do. I have seen pastors who say, "We really ought to do soul winning, we ought to do evangelism, we ought to reach out to our neighbor." But everyone knows their talk is merely an empty admonition, a hollow cliché, or an unaccomplished concept. A pastor becomes credible, however, who is able to say, "Here is someone whom I have led to Christ" or "Here is my next-door neighbor whom I have led to Christ." A leader who demonstrates what he or she proposes is always easier to follow than a mere theorist or a boisterous windbag. Credible leaders always strengthen the allegiance of followers when they can show effective results, especially in transformed lives.

• **Christlikeness.** A person who is a strong leader shows divine qualities. Such a leader has to keep close to God. People have confidence in him or her. They must believe she can do more for God than anyone else as their leader. The character issue in pastoral leaders is significantly more important than we sometimes think. Great pastors have a vital, up-to-date relationship with Christ, and it shows. That is the kind of pastor people want to follow.

TEMPTATIONS GREAT LEADERS MUST AVOID

I have had some personal disappointments with great pastoral leaders in my lifetime. Let me suggest six dangerous pitfalls to avoid. Any one of these temptations can ruin even the most effective leader.

1. **To forget the lesson of Judges.** Some pastors forget what I call the lesson of the Book of Judges. You remember how the people served the Lord all the days of Joshua and how the elders who outlived Joshua remembered the great work the Lord had done for them. But then the people began to leave the Lord. They served Him for one generation. The second generation began to drift. Then the third generation began to leave the Lord.

Richard Niebuhr has an insightful paradigm he called from rags to riches in three generations. The first generation begins with nothing, so they work hard, have great ethics, pull themselves up, and start a business. Their children, the second generation, live off Dad's values and hard work and continue to grow the business. But the third generation, no longer valuing the practices of their father and not knowing grandfather very well, depart from what built the business and destroy it. Then they have to start over again.

That is the pattern for many churches and Christian organizations. Churches that begin as a flame of God in the first generation become by the third generation an institution that has forgotten the Lord who raised them up in the first place.

This mistake is easy to make. Pastors sometimes forget where they started or what caused their churches to succeed in the first generation. They forget the lessons in Judges.

2. **To become too worldly-wise.** What bothers me are ministers who forget their personal holiness and neglect the spiritual factors of church growth. True greatness always declines when self-sufficiency and professional cynicism set in. Our Lord's teaching that we are to be in the world but not of the world must be kept uppermost in our perspective and practice. Keep growing as a Christian all the days of your life.

3. **To develop a messianic complex.** These pastors try to do everything. As the church grows, they never learn how to organize, administer, and manage a church. I was recently in an Independent Baptist church where the pastor was getting ready to retire, and he was incredibly frustrated. Amazingly, he got this church up to almost 2,000. He likes to boast, "All I have is a half-time secretary. I can pastor this church without additional staff." He has no janitors, no paid staff, and all these years he has been able to run this military church.

It takes two wings to fly, two legs to walk, and two rails on which to run a train.

Then he said, "I cannot find anyone to pastor this church. I am ready to retire, but I cannot find anyone to take this church for me." What a sad thing—his messianic complex created his problem and likely will create even more problems for many years ahead in that congregation.

4. **To neglect personal growth.** It takes two wings to fly, two legs to walk, and two rails on which to run a train. One rail is the spiritual factors and the other is natural factors. Of course, you must pray, be anointed, and lead worship; but you must also understand leadership, administration, management.

Many sad stories can be told of pastors who could gather lots of people but did not grow personally so as to maintain or expand the growth. Management skill is an example. Now management is basically four things: you manage time, people, facilities, and money. But as a church grows, managing those four resources keeps changing and becoming more complex.

I know a pastor who served a church for about 14 years. He had 175 attending when he came, and he still had 175 at the end of 14 years. He told me, "I have always let the people run the church. I just want to preach, but I have wondered why my preaching does not build the church." Then to avoid a midlife crisis, he went back to a state university and enrolled in an MBA program. Note his personal development discovery when he said, "I went with an open heart to learn everything I could about administration. In every class, I learned something I did wrong or did not do at all in my church."

Then he said, "Now I have a church of 400. My basic understanding of administration, discovering new ways of working with people, and learning how to manage have made the difference."

Other examples of personal growth issues might be in human relations, sociology studies to understand culture, communication for improved preaching and writing, or personal spiritual formation. Becoming a growing person increases your self-worth as well as your pastoral effectiveness.

5. **To practice self-deception.** Sometimes pastors lie to themselves. They deceive themselves about how big their church is. They fool themselves about what their Sunday School attendance is. They even lie to themselves about how good their church members are or how strong their marriage is. They have lost touch. Some lose touch with people they originally reached. There was a day when pastor and people were one, when they worked together on cleanup day. Once they were visiting together on outreach day. Once the pastor was a player coach, but now he has lost touch—no time or commitment to maintain the common touch.

I always feel sad when I hear a pastor's church has grown so large he does not do weddings, funerals, or hospital calling. I worked with Jerry Falwell, and I want you to know he will probably make as many hospital calls as any pastor you will ever meet. He wants to keep a personal contact with people. And he does.

Other self-deceptions ruin pastors when they do not establish a system of self-imposed accountability regarding their own spiritual, emotional, and physical health. Everyone needs reality checks about ministry, intentions, money, and marriage. The larger an organization gets, the harder it becomes for subordinates, staff members, and church members to tell the head leader of a fault or weakness they see in him or her. If you do have weaknesses, and you fail to discover and correct them, they may lead to a fatal failure.

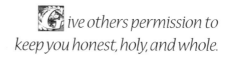

ive others permission to keep you honest, holy, and whole.

Give others permission to keep you honest, holy, and whole. Some pastors live their whole life in mediocrity because they refuse to discover the truth about themselves.

6. **To neglect the character issue.** Character is continually doing the right thing in the right way. Some surrender their principles as their church starts to grow. They give in to secular values or controllers with money, or they become expedient pragmatists. Such a decline does not need to happen.

Now, when we describe an encounter with greatness, who is the greatest man who ever lived? If you go back to the Old Testament, it could be Abraham, the father of the Jews, but it wasn't. It could be Moses, who gave the Law, but it wasn't. It could have been David, a man after God's own heart, but it wasn't.

When Jesus spoke about the greatest man to have ever lived, He named John the Baptist. John the Baptist is the greatest to have ever lived (Matt. 11:11). Why would Jesus say John is the greatest? Greatest in what capacity? He was great in moral character, a great reformer, great in introducing Jesus.

But notice an amazing announcement in Matt. 11:11b: "yet he who is least in the kingdom of heaven is greater than he [John]." According to Jesus, the greatest leader who ever lived could be you. The greatest leader to have ever been born of woman could come about in these last days. It could be someone who calls the Church and the world back to God. We think about the First Great Awakening and the Second Great Awakening, but there could be a Third Great Awakening. You could be the leader who is even greater than John the Baptist.

Hot Poker Philosophy for Forming Great Leaders

Back when I wrote the book *Ten Largest Sunday Schools,* I preached in 87 of the 100 largest churches in the United States as I did research for that book. In those churches, the leader would ask, "What is it going to take to build a great church? I would like to build one of the great churches in America."

In reply, I coined a phrase called the hot poker philosophy. The idea is to stick a poker into the fire to get it hot. The simple idea is to get next to leaders whose hearts are on fire for God. Then take on the heat, the warmth, the glow, and the flame of some of the greatest leaders you can find. There are four simple ways to do it.

● **Visit great places.** Every other year, I teach a D.Min. course in Korea. I go the first day to my Korean students and I say, "As soon as this class is over, I want four men to divide the city of Seoul, Korea, into zones and find the greatest churches in each zone. Before this course is over, I want us to visit every one of the large churches of Korea."

I assign them, "Phone and tell them we are coming. Ask the pastor if he could meet us, chat briefly with us. Tell him we are not going to stay long. Let's go visit four or five churches each day."

So I take my students to visit these great churches. When I walk in, I walk straight to the pulpit. Like buying a suit, I try it on. I stand in the pulpit; I pound a little bit, look up here, look up there, and then I quote, "Make a joyful noise unto the Lord." Then I will say to my students, "Yes, it will preach," and I walk away.

At first my students say, "Oh, no, no, no, no. Koreans are too shy." But before you know it, they will walk right up there with me.

Let me tell you the power of visiting great places. I have had those students tell me years later, "Do you remember going to the church and standing there?" And I say, "Yes." Then they say, "When I went to a large church and stood there, I prayed in my heart, 'O God, give me a church this large.'" Now, that is cultivating your vision. Every time you see a great church, walk in, stand in the pulpit, and pray for a greater vision.

• **Meet great people.** You'll learn greatness being around great people. Don't be bashful—have your spouse take your pic-

> *f God is going to let the Holy Spirit fall, do not get it on cassette tape. Be there.*

ture with them. Keep your picture so you can see yourself with Billy Graham, John Maxwell, or Rick Warren. Those people love preachers. Often they will stop whatever they are doing to share their heart with you.

• **Attend great meetings.** Seminars, conferences, conventions, and assemblies can change your life forever. If God is going to let the Holy Spirit fall, do not get it on cassette tape. Be there.

• **Read great books.** If you have not read *Pilgrim's Progress,* do it soon. Or read it again. Read *The Christian's Secret of a Happy Life* by Hannah Whitall Smith and *Revival Lectures* by Finney. Ask your heroes in ministry to recommend the books that have impacted them. Read from the best-seller list to understand your times. Set yourself up on a reading schedule.

Ten years from now you will be the product of the places you have been, the people you have met, and the books you have read.

THE SURE PATH TO GREATNESS

To become a great leader, try to make these wise words from *The Leader of the Future* by C. William Pollard, chairman of ServiceMaster Company, a part of your ministry: "A servant leader's results will be measured beyond the workplace, and the story will be told in the changed lives of others. There is no scarcity of feet to wash. The towels and the water are available. The limitation is our ability to get on our hands and knees and be prepared to do what we ask others to do."

The Greatest of the Great summarized the path to greatness in 10 words: "He that is greatest among you will be your servant" (Matt. 23:11, KJV).

9

WHAT WILL REMAIN AFTER YOU'RE GONE?

Using Integrity and Identity to Support the Vision

by Maxie D. Dunnam

Among the most unforgettable experiences of my ministry was a service of consecration to the Christian ministry for a young physician, Dr. Wilson Bonfin, in Rio de Janeiro. This inspiring event took place at the World Methodist Conference in 1996. Dr. Bonfin had become converted and felt the call of Christ to become an evangelist. Fortunately, a wise person showed him how he could connect medicine with being an evangelist and EvangeMed was born. In this unique ministry, this young doctor moves from village to village around Rio de Janeiro in a mobile clinic where he ministers to the medical needs of the people with a team of nurses and preaches the gospel to his patients.

The consecration service was such a meaningful experience to me because as this young man knelt, those persons laying hands on him were his pastor; his bishop; Eddie Fox, the director of World Evangelism; my successor at Christ Church in Memphis, Dr. Bill Bauknight; and me as chair of World Evangelism for the United Methodist Church. Bill Bauknight was there because Christ United Methodist Church contributed $70,000 to build the mobile clinic Dr. Bonfin will use in this project. This idea for EvangeMed became a reality because a church in Memphis, Tennessee, had a passion for the world. That consecration service for Dr. Bonfin was a verification of the ministry that was mine while I served Christ Church as pastor.

Let me fill in a few details of this beautiful picture. I started ministry at Christ Church, Memphis, Tennessee, in March of 1982. At that time, 2,800 folks were on the membership roll, but we had addresses for only 2,400. Then when I left to go to Asbury Seminary in 1994, the church had 6,200 members, had built $8 million worth of buildings, and owed less than $1 million. During my ministry we added two Sunday morning worship services and a Saturday night service, and our annual budget grew to $3.5 million.

> *rowth in worship, membership, mission, and outreach have not missed a beat.*

We were one of the best-known churches in that city because of our worship services, our spiritual growth groups, and our mission to the world. We also became one of the most outstanding churches in Methodism.

The thrilling thing is that these factors have not changed since I left but have become more pronounced. Growth in worship, membership, mission, and outreach have not missed a beat. My successor, Bill Bauknight, is providing remarkable leadership. Worship attendance continues to grow. Membership is over 6,500. They just made a commitment to expand their buildings at a cost of $10 million. And they plan to tithe that $10 million to missions; $70,000 has already been given for that mobile clinic in the EvangeMed project in Brazil. That all came together for me when I was privileged to lay hands on Dr. Wilson Bonfin to consecrate him for that ministry.

I hope you can faintly imagine my inexpressible joy. For all of us, what remains is a serious issue of ministry. What remains after we are gone really tells the story of what we did in a place. What will remain after you are gone is dependent upon the integrity of your life and the quality of your ministry out of which your vision grows.

You Can Choose "Sellout" over "Burnout"

Let me begin with this assertion—a pastor can choose to sell out or burn out. These days we hear a lot about a serious hazard of ministry called burnout. Certainly burnout is an issue that needs discussion, and we must develop practical ways to prevent it from happening. But I want to sound two warnings that I firmly believe are fully as threatening as burnout.

First is the danger of turning our ministry into a career rather than a calling, a profession rather than a vocation.

Now I do not mean we are not to be professional in conduct and appearance. Becoming genuine professionals is one of the reasons for having the Beeson Institute for Advanced Church Leadership. That is a reason why Asbury Theological Seminary is trying to be the best seminary it can possibly become; we want to provide professional tools for well-trained persons in ministry. We should be as accomplished in what we do as a competent medical doctor or an accomplished lawyer.

But there is a vast difference between being professional in the way we do ministry and making ministry into a profession or turning our calling into a career. Henri Nouwen made a strong case for this difference in *The Living Reminder* when he wrote, "Profession as we conceive of it today primarily suggests training, skill, expertise, and a certain specialization. Theological education in recent decades has made a major contribution toward establishing the ministry as a profession in a highly professionalized world, but *profession* also refers to professing, witnessing, proclaiming, announcing. This professing side of our ministerial life, which is deeply rooted in our biblical heritage, requires spiritual formation as well. Profession as expertise and profession as proclamation can never be separated without harm."

When Nouwen continues, he underscores the disquieting crux of the issue: "When we profess our faith in Christ without any ministerial expertise, we are like people shouting from the mountaintop without caring if anyone is listening. But when we are skillful experts who have little to profess, then we easily become lukewarm technicians who squeeze God's work between 9 A.M. and 5 P.M."

Ours is a vocation, a calling—a calling to serve Christ and His world. It is not a career or a profession. We must remember we are ministers by divine commission. In Col. 1:25, Paul says it clearly: "I have been made a minister." Another did the choosing. God chose us. Then the apostle becomes even more explicit when he says in verse 25 of the first chapter of Colossians, "I am a minister by divine commission" (PHILLIPS). There is danger in turning our ministry into a career where we put in a 40-hour week and are not moved by the deep needs of people.

We must remember we are ministers by divine commission.

I had a marvelous experience recently of hearing one of the great leaders of the church. In fact, he is among the most respected world leaders in the Wesleyan Methodist movement. I am speaking of Bishop William R. Connon, now retired and in his 80s. When the confession movement started in the United Methodist Church, Bishop Connon was invited to present an address at a national gathering. Those who arranged the meeting asked him to give a kind of an apologetic for the Christian faith because many of us feel that the faith is being tested and challenged in mainline churches today. Get the picture of this frail man, who can hardly stand, leaning over the lectern making a brilliant apologetic for the Christian faith. His address was one of the most moving messages I have ever heard.

Bishop Connon closed by sharing a personal testimony. He told about being converted at age seven. He talked about the family of his birth—a family peopled by lawyers, doctors, distinguished judges, and merchants. He explained how his family naturally expected him to follow in their footsteps. Then he said with amazing conviction, "When I was converted at age seven, it wasn't as though the Lord called me to preach in the way that we normally talk about that. But rather I offered myself to the Lord to be one of His ministers." He continued, "The Lord accepted me. And I never wanted to be anything else but a preacher of the gospel; I have not been disobedient to that heavenly vision."

It is that conviction of call and obedience to the heavenly vision that keeps our souls on fire. That is what keeps us centered on Christ and makes us refuse to turn our calling into a career. It enables us to be professional in our calling, but it is always a calling from Almighty God. Putting us in the ministry was God's idea, and that explains what we are about.

The second danger is a twin concern—perhaps the other side of the same coin. It is a cynicism or skepticism that sets in. It is a loss of appetite for ministry, especially with people who have professionalized their ministry. If you are observant, you see it all around you.

In fact, I believe this cynical "I've seen it all before" attitude and "nothing can change" spirit is a primary problem in the church today. I believe many pastoral leaders do their jobs well but without passion, fervor, or intensity. They are part of a system more than a significant minister of Christ's kingdom. So they learn how the system works and they work the system. They play the game to their advantage, and they play the game well. They run their churches effectively. Their people accept them, but little

Putting us in the ministry was God's idea, and that explains what we are about.

is happening that transforms or redeems. There is no sitting on the edge of their seat, anticipating what God is going to do next in the congregation. There is no stretching themselves. There is no fire in their belly. There is no attempt to do things they know will fail unless they are empowered by the Holy Spirit.

The danger I fear is a cynicism in those who do the job well but without a do-or-die commitment like every forward-moving Kingdom enterprise deserves and demands.

Warning Signs

These two dangers—turning our calling into a career and losing our appetite for ministry—are both connected with burnout. But they are also tightly connected with our relationship to God. Let me note some warning signs that arise when we allow a distance to develop between God and us.

• "I have lost heart for ministry"

When we lose heart for ministry, zest for Christ burns low, if we ever had it. You know the feeling—you just face another counseling session to endure, another hospital visit to make, and another sermon to prepare.

- **"I feel depressed about my own spirituality"**

  I am referring to feeling depressed about my own spirituality for a significant period of time. I am not talking about blue Mondays or a week of dryness. Rather I have in mind an extended period of time when we are depressed about our own relation to the Holy.

- **"My decisions are not thought through"**

  We are on automatic pilot. Ministers can get good at doing things mechanically, without thought and with little deep feeling or no concern. That's the time to stop, to reflect, to check it out, to test ourselves in light of why God put us in ministry.

  Why is personal renewal so difficult to address and follow through on?

- **"My emotions are off base, inappropriate"**

  This warning shows when emotions do not fit the demands and events. If I am attentive, I can tell it in the way I answer the phone. I do not want to talk on the phone, and if I talk, I am not listening. My emotions are off kilter. I get angry too easily. I am too quick to judge or there is easy an acceptance in myself and others of that which is wrong.

- **"I have a chronic problem with sleeplessness"**

  I do not mean those times when the Lord keeps us awake. I believe the serious servant of Christ is sometimes kept awake at night. But this warning comes when distance from the Lord and boredom in ministry produce persistent sleep difficulties.

Hindrances to a Visionary Leader

So these are some of the signs that warn you about a growing distance from the Lord. Now, many of us know all of this from personal experience. Why, then, do people like us struggle so much or even resist personal renewal? Why is personal renewal so difficult to address and follow through on?

There are many hindering forces that prevent us from pursuing renewal and from becoming visionaries through renewal.

But I especially want to underscore four commonplace obstacles to renewal among ministers.

• **Fear of failure.** Management consultant Kets deVries, in his book *Prisoners of Leadership,* calls this the "f dimension"—or the failure factor. Now this is a matter of ego, a large problem with many pastors. None of us wants to fail, so a crippling fear of failure causes us to spend too much time and energy on an organizational agenda and on the church as an institution. As a result, we do not pay enough attention to our inner life, to our family wholeness, and to our own spirituality. In the process, we become a generic leader of an organization rather than really becoming a faith-energized Christian leader. So, our fear of failure drives us to the point that we fail to pay attention to what is lacking in our personal lives.

I have been reflecting on this fear phenomenon, which I think is a telling one in our culture and in our churches. It is amazing to me that personal disasters and family failures—divorce, for example—are becoming more and more acceptable among Christian leaders. Personal family failures are becoming more acceptable while failures in ministry are less acceptable among people like us.

Then, too, none of us wants a church to fail during our term of service. Now, that's not all bad, but when a fear of failure drives us to a point that dominates all that we are and all that we do, then we are not going to seek that spiritual personal renewal we need.

• **Inappropriate ambition or hunger for prestige.** A second hindrance that prevents us from pursuing renewal and becoming visionary is inappropriate ambition or prestige. There is a sense in which this is connected with our fear of failure. But it is also somewhat different from that. Our drive for promotion and the prestige we think might come from moving to a bigger assignment prevent us from paying attention to our present assignment and our own personal renewal. Hunger for prestige, power, and position is hard to admit to God or even to ourselves.

Let's face reality; chances are you are not going to stay in the church you now serve for the rest of your ministry. Knowing that, letting that fact become a dominant force in how you orient your life is easy. Here's how it works. As you thirst for prestige that would come if you moved to some more desirable or attractive assignment, you begin thinking of clever or even scheming ways to make that happen. You almost unconsciously think of ways you can get that move. Before long, you try those approaches.

unger for prestige, power, and position is hard to admit to God or even to ourselves.

● **Overachievement.** Something strange occurs when the move you wanted does not materialize. Not given the opportunity for promotion, many of us think we will not be recognized unless we overachieve in our present assignment. So we drive ourselves or others. Sometimes we drive ourselves mercilessly without any attempt to test our presuppositions or keep an accurate perspective. This is the pride of life the apostle John discusses in 1 John 2. Such overachieving almost always takes a terrible toll on our spouse, children, church members, and ourselves.

● **Job pressure.** The daily pressure of our jobs is another source of possible hindrance to personal renewal. The work of ministry can wear us down. The daily grind of ministry can keep us from becoming visionary in our leadership. All of you know that leadership responsibilities are so complex that more time is always needed just to stay on top of the job that is ours. We move from one thing after another; the pressure of the immediate—the "right now"—and our inability to put pressing current demands into perspective really throw us off track.

All of us need to find time to move outside the ongoing day-to-day pressures, to do the dreaming and visioning and getting into perspective the issues of our life. We need time and space to dream for renewal and for shaping our vision.

● **Greed.** This barrier to personal renewal is not so easy to identify. Greed gets to us. Now I'm not talking about an insatiable desire for things and monetary success, though there are pastors who take too many outside speaking engagements for the honorariums they receive. Others fret all their days about their own low salaries or how much money they think others make. To be sure, the normal kind of greed—wanting things for ourselves, therefore doing all those things that will bring things, including money, for ourselves—is an issue. That kind of greed often kills spiritual development.

But I am actually thinking about something quite different. It seems as though one of the unspoken rules of an organization is that enough is never enough. We always need more—better and bigger buildings, more programs, more staff, and on and on it goes. So we get into the kind of lifestyle of giving ourselves unstintingly, even sacrificially, to see that "more" might be achieved. What we might need to do is to have a bit less and enhance the quality of what we have.

Character brings stability to life and ministry.

Notice, then, how this affects the burnout issue. Every pastor can choose to sell out or burn out.

Of course, I am happy when the church I serve grows, when ministry expands, when what I do is "successful." But I have learned to see that as secondary. What really sustains my life and ministry is God, and the closer I am to Him, the more fruitful and satisfying is my work for Him.

When a pastor is sold out to Christ and sold out to ministry as a God-called vocation, he or she must seek to keep a crystal-clear differentiation between generic leadership used by business leaders and Christ-directed church leadership. That is the beginning of an inner integrity of life and a wholesome identity as a minister that provide the soil out of which visionary leadership grows and flourishes.

FIND IDENTITY IN WHO YOU ARE

Your public identity comes from the nature of your calling, your biblical understandings, and your personal faith roots. But your personal identity must be rooted in who you really are.

All the permanent fruits and lasting progress that result from your leadership are based on strong character. Character brings stability to life and ministry. Character makes a person an inspiring example for others. Character guides sound decisions and gives moral authority. God is more interested in who you are than in what you do. Nothing can happen *through* you that has not happened *to* you.

There's a marvelous story about Leontyne Price, a great woman who is recognized as a world-class operatic soprano voice. She comes from Laurel, Mississippi, 30 miles from my hometown of Richton. Coming from a deprived culture, she became a symbol of hope for thousands of people as she rose to the pinnacle of musical excellence—the Metropolitan Opera.

Much to the surprise of many, in the prime of her career after having been in the limelight for a couple of decades, she virtually disappeared from the stage of the Metropolitan Opera. In an interview, she discussed the reason for her more selective scheduling of recitals. She sounded like an authentic woman who knew who she was and where she was going when she said, "There are certain things in life that you have to have, because without them you are so uptight and tense that all the joy is gone from your performing. A few years ago, I could not have sat here talking with a critic, let alone talk about myself. I even used to assume conductors knew more than I did about my voice and work. Now . . ." Listen to this, "Now I have recaptured the joy of singing, the feeling that courses through your body when you know the tone is right and your whole being vibrates with it."

What Miss Price discovered in her art is what we must recover for our life in ministry. We must find and cherish a place where the harmony of the inner and the outer worlds resonate so we are one with it. We must recapture the joy of ministry and the feeling that vibrates in our soul when the tone is just right and the Sovereign Lord is well-pleased.

How Power and Influence Impact Vision

It is almost impossible to become a visionary leader with identity and integrity without thinking about the nature of influence and power. A working definition of *power* is the capability of doing or affecting something. This definition strongly implies the ability to influence others. How we use power determines whether we have integrity.

According to Kast and Rosenzweig, in *Rediscovering the Soul of Leadership* by Eugene B. Habecker, there are three kinds of power: physical power, material power, and symbolic power. Physical power is more readily thought of in the context of the police or a military organization. These types of entities have the power to harm, incarcerate, or even in certain circumstances to take one's life. An example of material power could be the leading financier of an organization. Any CEO knows the power of a donor who insists on using a donation to manipulate the organization toward a particular direction or to pursue a particular purpose. An example of symbolic power would be the ability to motivate people to do their best in order to help the organization achieve its goals.

John Gardner, quoted in the same book, provides useful analyses on the subject of power. He notes as follows: "Power is not to be confused with status or prestige. It is the capacity to ensure the outcomes one wishes and to prevent those one does not wish. Power as we are now speaking of it—power in the social dimension—is simply the capacity to bring about certain intended consequences in the behavior of others."

The issue for the Christian leader is how to use power. We always need to keep in mind the fact that there is a significant difference between generic and Christian leadership. And all of this relates to the whole question of this chapter: what will remain after you are gone?

What we want to be left is a Christian church—a church that is alive in its devotion to Jesus Christ, passionate about sharing the gospel, committed to demonstrating care and concern for people. We want to leave behind places of hospitality where the marginalized and the outcast and the troubled and the forsaken can find a place of welcome. We want to leave behind, in the best sense of the word, an authentic Christian community.

Since there is a marked sense that what we leave behind is a reflection of who we are, that leads me to this final section: you must allow spiritual formation to enhance who you are.

YOU CAN ALLOW SPIRITUAL FORMATION TO ENHANCE WHO YOU ARE

We are hearing a lot in our day about reinventing the organization and reinventing business. Al Gore has talked a lot about, and, in fact, is spending a lot of energy in what he calls "reinventing government."

In Kingdom efforts, however, we must think more about reinventing the self. That is an ongoing, necessary process if we

> *We must think more about reinventing the self.*

are going to have the integrity of life and ministry out of which vision grows. There are two dimensions to this ongoing reinventing of the self: memory and faith.

A neurologist in New York, Dr. Oliver Sacks, has written a book with the intriguing title *The Man Who Mistook His Wife for a Hat*. It is a book about his patients in a hospital in New York who have lost their memory because of severe amnesia, most of them because of a rare disease that is known as Korsakov's disease. Its symptoms are so debilitating that the patients have to be hospitalized and cared for for the rest of their lives.

Dr. Sacks writes about a man in his hospital named Mr. Thompson. Mr. Thompson's world is constantly in a flux, always moving. He was a grocer for a while. Then he was a minister, and then a mechanic, and then he was something else. Because there is no memory, there is no identity. He has to make up his world as he goes along, including his identity. It has taken its toll on him. He is tired all the time, and haggard, and always tense, always moving. He can never sit still. Dr. Sacks writes, "His world is reduced to a surface. It was brilliant, shimmering, ever changing, but still a surface. A mass of illusion, a delirium without depth." Then Dr. Sacks writes this: "Is this what it means to lose your soul?" (From a sermon by Rev. Mark Trotter titled "How Is Your Memory?" preached November 10, 1996, at the First United Methodist Church, San Diego, California.)

There is a lesson here. If a person who cannot remember the past is in the grip of a serious disease, what about the minister, the leader, who does not remember the soil out of which he or she has been grown? Can the minister lose his or her soul by failing to remember?

> *Memory is so important in reinventing the self.*

That is the reason that I have made such a case for remembering who we are as those who have been called, those who are who we are because of a divine commission.

Memory is so important in reinventing the self.

And, likewise faith—not only remembering who we are but keeping in mind that the God we serve is the One who makes all things new. He is the One who is constantly calling us on to join Him in His kingdom enterprise. It is when we keep memory and faith in dynamic tension that we can engage in the ongoing process of reinventing the self.

And as it relates to faith—as well as it relates to memory—our core value must be that of being alive in Christ.

Dale Galloway makes a strong case that a church goes through all sorts of stages and something new is needed or demanded at every stage in its development. Something new is required that has not been demanded in the past. And he is right. Among these new demands for a church, I believe, is the need for a new leader. The new leader is you—a new pastor who leads on and helps a congregation make the needed paradigm shift to do what God is calling this congregation to become and do.

Consider a searching question—can a congregation lose its soul? Can a local church become so preoccupied with its own agenda and so satisfied with serving its own people that its soul is in serious danger? Can a church become so successful in its own eyes that it loses contact with the passion and demands of the Christian gospel? Can a church really be a church with no desire to take the next leap into some Kingdom level of risk?

We are having a lot of those problems with memory in the United Methodist Church. Episcopalians, Presbyterians, Disciples, and Lutherans are having similar problems with memory loss. As you know, there is talk all over the place among mainline denominations about schism. We have lost memory. We do not see ourselves connected with the Day of Pentecost, when the Spirit descended and the Church was born. We do not see ourselves connected with historic times of renewal when our own denomination found itself at a place where it had responded to God's call upon its life. We see no connection to times when something new happened and something different started. We have lost our memory as denominations and as local congregations.

But what does it mean to think seriously about vigorous faith? Being who God called us to be and serving the One who makes all things new is a faith question. The One who is constantly calling us to join Him in a Kingdom enterprise requires and enables faith.

When was the last time the congregation you serve attempted something so bold, so demanding, so Kingdomlike that you knew you would fail unless you were the recipient of a power not your own? When did your congregation put itself on the line so everyone realized that unless the Holy Spirit enabled you to accomplish what you set out to do, the church would fail or at least be badly embarrassed? We as Christian congregations ought always to be moving in a direction that we cannot go unless we are guided and empowered by the Holy Spirit. All this relates to faith. When we talk about core values, let us be sure to include faith.

Let me say it loud and clear: the core value of the Christian faith is our being alive in Christ. I believe that the presence of God in Jesus Christ is not to be experienced only on occasion; the indwelling Christ is to become the shaping power of our lives.

I further believe that the two most crucial concepts in the New Testament—I would call them the core doctrines of the Christian faith—are (1) justification by grace through faith and (2) the possibility and power of the indwelling Christ. We must never diminish or falter in our passion for the core evangelical truth: we are justified by grace through faith. But we have not given the attention deserved to this equally fantastic truth of the Christian gospel: the indwelling Christ.

Off and now on for 25 years, my daily exercise has been to emphasize a word of faith to myself. Sometimes I speak it aloud. Sometimes I simply register it in my awareness. Sometimes I turn it into a liturgy. Sometimes I use it as an exercise, breathing in and breathing out. The word is this, "Christ *in you!* Yes,

Christ *in you,* bringing with him the hope of all the glorious things to come." That is J. B. Phillips' translation of Col. 1:27. I believe it is addressed to me personally, and I believe that stands at the heart of the Christian faith and Christian life.

> *f you want a definition of spiritual formation that builds faith, it is Christ at work in you.*

I believe the presence of God in Jesus Christ is not to be experienced only on certain lofty and sporadic occasions. The indwelling Christ is to become the shaping power of our daily existence. If you want a definition of spiritual formation that builds faith, it is Christ at work in you. Then spiritual formation is that dynamic process of receiving by faith and appropriating by commitment, discipline, and action the living Christ into our lives to the end that our lives will be conformed to and manifest the presence of our Lord in the world.

The dynamic of spiritual formation transforms both our inner and outer witness. This dynamic enables us to know that "the tone is right." But spiritual formation does not happen accidentally. It demands commitment and discipline. Not to pay attention to our spiritual formation and that of our congregations is perhaps the greatest failure of pastors.

I want to briefly share two essential disciplines that are especially appropriate for today and for making our leadership visionary and Christ-centered. These disciplines help develop and inform the integrity of life that is essential for leaving something worthwhile and lasting behind. Of course, we want to pray, to worship, to receive holy Communion, and to read Scripture. But there are two others.

One discipline is what John Wesley called Christian conferencing. Check it out. Many leaders fail because they do not make themselves accountable. Spiritual accountability means telling each other our stories of struggle and faith. This is self-imposed accountability where we share our dreams with each other and where we check them out as far as the Spirit is concerned. My conviction is that you will not succeed the way God wants you to until accountability becomes a serious and self-imposed commitment of your life.

The second discipline for effective spiritual formation is what I call acting our way into Christlikeness. I have never seen a person who studied himself or herself into Christlikeness. Neither have I seen a person who prayed or worshiped his or her way into Christlikeness. I have, however, seen countless people behave their way into Christlikeness. Of course, they prayed, they worshiped, and they studied, but they also became like Jesus because they acted like Him. The greatest of all accolades is to have someone say, "He [or she] acts like Jesus."

What Do You Want to Remain After You Are Gone?

A young Roman Catholic man who was a member of a religious order asked for an interview with Mother Teresa. He shared his frustrations that his order was putting too much pressure on him to do routine organizational tasks that had to be done at the monastery. He complained, "I just can't do it. I'm committed to serving lepers. My vocation is to serve lepers. And not to serve in the monastery."

Mother Teresa looked at him with those piercing eyes and faint smile. Then she said, "Young man, your vocation is not to serve lepers. Your vocation is to belong to and to love Jesus."

That is our vocation. That is our calling. When we become so passionate about belonging to and loving Jesus, something happens in our ministry that makes a lasting difference. It will make a difference in the world, in the church, and in your own life. It will encourage others to faithfulness where it counts. It will stimulate a healthy memory of the Christian story so one day the kingdoms of this world will become the kingdoms of Christ. Then He shall reign forever and ever.

Being successful and using power like the world may build a flourishing congregation, but it will not necessarily keep your name written in the Lamb's Book of Life. Integrity of life and ministry is grounded in our personal relationship to Jesus Christ. The closer we get to Him, the more we will act like Him; then the Church we lead will look and act more like Him.

That's a great and eternal enterprise to lead. Don't forget who you are and who called you. Get a crystal-clear focus on what you want to leave behind. Commit to Christlikeness and live in the delights of being indwelled by Him.